The Missing Piece In Bouncing Back

Inspiring Stories
From Amazing People

Compiled By Nicky Marshall

Seathorne Walk

Bridlington

East Yorkshire, YO16 7QP

England

For information visit www.themissingpiecepublishing.com

Book and Cover Design by Jennifer Insignares

www.yourdesignsbyjen.com

ISBN: 978-1-63452-986-0

Gratitude & Appreciation

There are so many people to thank right now. I'm really feeling the love!

To Kate and 'The Missing Piece' team: You have been there at every step finding solutions, cheering me on, shaping this book, and bringing your professionalism, thank you.

To my amazing Co-authors: Thank you for sharing your stories and trusting me to bring this book together! You have all been so supportive and risen above your personal challenges, bravo!

To my wonderful family: Having a family like ours is pretty special. When I was younger, I didn't really appreciate that this isn't always the norm. I include my close friends as part of my soul family, so this is for you too. Thank you for your support, love, sense of humour, and your belief. You cheer me on and kick my behind as needed, and for both, I love you all!

To Mum, Ami and Kassi: Thank you for adding your stories and energy to this book, I have shed many tears in the editing process!

Nicky Marshall

Table of Contents

Introduction

Wow, have you seen? We have a book!

My decision to bring 24 people together was made in an excited, 'off the cuff' way with no real idea of what I was starting…but I think most inspirational adventures start like that.

Roll back to 26th July 2010 and the day that would change the rest of my life…I could have used that diving accident to sit back and give up, to close my business and take up basket weaving. Instead I used it as my launchpad, my path back to health and wellbeing and a continuous journey of improvement. I did it for me, I did it for my family and I did it to prove I could serve people in a deep and meaningful way.

Discover Your Bounce was also born in an 'off the cuff' way. The whole programme came to me over three, 3am sessions where a voice was shouting at me to get up. My wonderful mother-in-law had lost her battle with cancer a few weeks earlier and I know in my heart that she helped me write it.

So I had a six-part system and a name – would it work? Would it help the people that I saw struggling every day? Would it help the heroes and heroines that go about their lives being there for others, giving their time and energy and all the while suffering with health concerns, lack of sleep, gaps in confidence and years of being suppressed?

The elements of this system had enabled me to gain full health as well as regaining my diving medical after a muscular, skeletal and cerebral bend that had also caused a stroke. A complete recovery within 3 years when the prognosis had been, "How you are in 18 months is how you will be for the rest of your life." Diving again had been an impossible dream and now it is a reality.

I decided to ask for a couple of people to test the system out for me – and boy did it work! The testimonials started rolling in and for me it was so special watching wonderful humans achieving more, while feeling great in the process.

The last two years have been incredible; I now have six 'Bounce Creators' that have joined my team. Licensees who are training people in Bounce techniques. We have a super brand full of energy, a beautiful website and a plan to allow Discover Your Bounce to grow into the 'go to' company for wellbeing and happiness.

The idea of the book came from the amazing people I have met. We all go through challenges in life; loss, struggle, illness and trauma in one guise or another. I thought it would be inspirational to have a collection of stories from real people, so that others would feel like they weren't alone. I wanted someone to read the book and think, "If someone else has gone through it and bounced back to live happier and more fully then why can't I?"

As the authors appeared and the chapters were written the energy started to grow. Once the cover appeared and I started to read the chapters the energy grew even more. Our author group has become a band of friends, cheering each other on and lending support when the writer's block hit or a deadline loomed.

I cried as I read the struggles and stories of people, some I knew well and others I had just met. I smiled at the humour and support. I began to love the group that had come together and I was humbled at the part I was playing.

Now that this beautiful book is in existence the next chapter begins. My hope is that while we may be moved to tears by the struggles, we will be uplifted by the outcomes. Life is about light and shade, but my hope for all of us is that the light outweighs the shade and that in shady moments we all have someone to reach for.

I want this book to become a well-thumbed friend; a regular feature on the coffee tables of doctors and dentists, of solicitors and counsellors. I want this little book to grow a life of its own and make its way into the world, to be shared and to discover some bounce!

Wishing you toe-curling, grin spreading happiness!

Nicky Marshall

International Bestselling Author, Speaker, Mentor and Founder of Discover Your Bounce

www.discoveryourbounce.com

Nicky Marshall

Nicky has a unique talent for breaking down the barriers that hold you back in life and giving you the confidence, energy and passion to live the life of your dreams.

After suffering a stroke and fully recovering within 3 years, Nicky walks her talk and can hold your hand through your 'bouncing back' process. She has 7 books in publication with more in the pipeline, she hosts retreats, is a speaker and a mentor – so pick your method for change!

Nicky has passion in buckets, she loves to inspire, she gives great hugs and she's a good listener. Nicky's knowledge, knack for stress-busting and infectious laugh is a favourite combination with entrepreneurs aiming for success.

You can reach Nicky at:

Website:
www.discoveryourbounce.com

Facebook:
www.facebook.com/discoveryourbounce
www.facebook.com/nickymarshallauthor

Twitter:
www.twitter.com/bounce2success

YouTube:
https://www.youtube.com/channel/UCBXK2Ut7IyL39-Pc1cRr2lA

Failing To Succeed
By Nicky Marshall

Have you ever failed at something and felt your stomach sink? Have you ever had someone say to you, "How's business?" and answered with words and a smile that were fake?

I know I have.

You see I have walked the path of the entrepreneur, but in the beginning I had no idea that this was the route I had chosen.

I am a bright, educated, intelligent woman. I started my career in finance and spent 10 years learning about money. I am a Management Accountant after re-training once my girls came along, so I really know about money!

I have a strong and supportive family who encourage me to reach for my dreams, so when I decided to start my own business, although they were concerned that I was walking away from a good salary (which admittedly came at the price of my confidence and peace of mind), they wished me all the luck in the world.

My nickname in the early days was 'The Puppy'. Once I had an idea that was it, I was off in full-speed-ahead mode getting everything started. I had passion in heaps and wanted the whole wide world to know the benefits of using holistic therapies and following your intuition. I was evangelical, energetic and completely chaotic looking back.

I started by renting a room for my therapies and attending Mind, Body and Spirit events. Later I organised these events myself.

Each one would have a catchy name, amazing graphics and I would work tirelessly; but at the end of every one I would put on my accountant head and compile a spreadsheet. This was the heart sinking moment – all that work and no money.

There were other failings too. My therapies and events were evenings and weekends whereas my husband worked 6am – 3pm. This was husband number two and I loved him so much all I wanted to do was be with him. Instead we were like ships passing in the kitchen – one in, one out. Was my business ever going to succeed if I was wishing I was at home?

As if the Universe heard my wishes I had the opportunity of setting up a therapy centre in a 3 way partnership. Again The Puppy was off, enthusiastically setting all systems to go with arrangements, Ikea purchases, wild ideas of events and happiness at having a base.

Again it worked…to a point. At 3 months in when 12 hour, 7 day weeks took their toll our relationship as partners fell apart. With no partnership agreement (who needs one of those, we're new best friends, right?) everything got messy and the ending of this business nearly took my sanity too.

I sat at home and licked my wounds. I listened to the mental chatter telling me of my shortcomings, flaws and wrong doings. I may as well have spent every day of that 3 months having coffee and buying shoes…I would have had more to show for it!

After some wallowing, I picked myself up, dusted myself off and got on with it. As I say I come from a supportive family so there were hugs, cups of tea and kindly words that shook off any feelings of pity for my situation. I set about finding somewhere to work from that was close to home and affordable where I could work school hours now that my children were approaching their final exams.

Once again the Universe delivered.

While buying a tent for my daughter's birthday the perfect space appeared. Two tiny joined conservatories on a small business estate with a café nearby. I had always had a dream of a holistic coffee shop and this was near enough for me. I had a therapy and reading room and a small shop selling crystal jewellery and I was in heaven.

After 7 months I felt ready for a new adventure and found another perfect space – my very own coffee shop! I had been dreaming of this since I started in business. For years I had uttered the words, "When I have my holistic coffee shop…" I knew the coffee we would serve, the cakes we would choose and how the space would be…every detail was alive in my mind's eye.

On the 10th April 2010 we opened our doors and again The Puppy surfaced! The stakes were high this time – this was my dream business after all. The decisions I had made about working to suit my lifestyle were forgotten and soon the evening and weekend working returned, but this time with full days too. The passion that I had in buckets sustained me for a while, but then the cracks started to appear.

My husband Phil is a saint and knew I loved my business, but I knew I was neglecting him and this made me sad. On days when my children were ill I was stuck manning the shop when my heart wanted to be with them giving them cuddles (even grown-ups need their Mummy when they are ill!).

My health suffered so badly that on a routine dive 3 months later I had a diving accident that caused a stroke. What followed was a long recovery period - a story to be told in another book I feel! We kept the shop going, but it was time and energy intensive and although this was my dream, the reality still lacked the magical elements I needed to be happy.

Once again I admitted failure and sold my shop. The money had been ok, but the overheads were high and the personal life price even higher. Somehow though this one didn't seem as hard to deal with. The voice on my shoulder didn't berate me or drag my feelings through the dirt, as there was inspiration coming to light about everything I had done so far.

Of course my stroke recovery had taught me much and the soul searching that went on had helped my inner calm. In addition my years as a business owner were now paying rewards.

Where are we today?

Discover Your Bounce is a programme that creates wellbeing and happiness. It works for everyone, young and old, but the majority of my clients are, you guessed it, entrepreneurs!

You see I now know the life of the entrepreneur. They call it a Hero's Journey for very good reason. You are driven by a passion and no other way will do. You know you can make a difference to the world and could not return to a 9-5 job, ever. Period.

Here's the most important thing. Every time I thought I was failing, I was actually succeeding. I was finding out who I am. I learned my strengths. I know my values. I gained new skills. I followed those who have gone before me and added my own talents.

I know what I don't want too – and sometimes that is an excellent place to start!

When you are travelling the country wishing you were at home your business will not work. When you are working out of your back bedroom yearning for the freedom of the open road that won't work either. If you are a night owl dragging yourself to morning networking you won't have the energy to create relationships and neither will morning people at evening events.

When you align your values, your skills and your hours with that great idea then you have found your recipe for success.

This great quote has really struck a chord with me:

"To succeed in life, you need three things: a wishbone, a backbone, and a funny bone." ~ Reba McEntire

Strength, aspiration and a sense of humour are the three things I wish I had consciously deployed when I started out on this journey. Laughing at our own frailties remind us that we are human and also engages the frontal lobe of the brain to solve problems. A backbone is needed when our fear grips us so that we keep on keeping on. As for a wishbone, well you can see how, when I knew what I wanted, the Universe repeatedly delivered.

When we are crystal clear on what we are setting out to achieve, the cogs and wheels stir to get us to our goals. When something doesn't work there is always a lesson in there too – what key element was missing that stopped the magic from happening?

Look back over your own life. Every time you 'failed' was there something beautiful that happened? Did you learn a new skill that proved invaluable on your next step?

Never be afraid to have a go, to take a step and give that thing a try, whatever it is. Trust that you will know if it's right and listen to your inner voice when really you know it's not for you. Try not to carry on regardless, be bold and brave and make your changes – your future self will thank you!

My mission is to help people who have a dream and keep it inside. I see people who are miserable where they are and think they have no choice. By having a go and even publicly failing, you give others inspiration by seeing that they don't have to be perfect. When they see you laugh at your early efforts and end up at a place of success they too may take that first step. They may even learn from you and not fail at all!

Ami Marshall

Ami is in her mid-20s, living in Bristol with her fiancé Tom. She has a wicked sense of humour and is passionate about living life on her own terms.

In 2013 after a long journey of chronic pain, fatigue and illness, Ami was diagnosed with endometriosis. A number of surgeries, lifestyle and diet changes later Ami is almost pain-free. She now helps others on a similar path to overcome pain and misinformation through her blog and by coaching people through the 'Discover Your Bounce' programme.

In her free time she enjoys cooking things from scratch, reading and spending time with loved ones.

You can reach Ami at:
Blog:
http://www.amimarshall.blogspot.com

Twitter:
http://www.twitter.com/Endo_Goddess

Facebook:
http://www.facebook.com/AmiMarshallEcoGoddess

Website:
http://www.discoveryourbounce.com/online/?ref=2

Giving In But Not Giving Up
By Ami Marshall

Everyone has at least one day in their life that changes everything – Tuesday 30th July 2013 was that day for me. After another day of being dismissed by the medical profession I broke down in tears in Mum's kitchen.

"I give in." I told her. "If someone else wants to fight this battle for me, I won't stop them. I give in. I can't do it myself anymore."

Things change when you give in, sometimes with alarming speed. Within minutes I was white, vomiting and had an emergency appointment booked with a different doctor to my usual one. Within hours I was packing my bags for the hospital and by midnight I'd been admitted with two very serious infections.

Let's back up a bit though, about 6 months to be precise. Although I'd always suffered irregular, painful periods I'd put it down as normal and got on with life. It wasn't until January 2013 that things started getting worse – the pain was starting earlier, lasting longer and affecting my daily life more. I was starting to experience other symptoms; back and rib pain, bloating, IBS-like symptoms and extreme fatigue.

This was the start of a 6 month dance with my doctor – at first I was given stronger painkillers, but as the pain started to last all month she moved on to an IBS diagnosis. We went through a number of diet changes, medications and promises of seeing a specialist (the last one never materialised), but nothing was working.

The pain kept getting more intense. By March I was sleeping on the living room floor for 2 hours a night so as not to wake Tom up, spending the rest of my time working out the maximum painkillers I could take and scalding myself with hot water bottles because only the most intense heat could give me relief.

Luckily at this time I was working in Mum's business and she was very accommodating. As long as the work got done it didn't matter if I was curled up in a ball with a hot water bottle strapped to my stomach. Being able to work this way meant I was still able to support myself... most of the time.

Even though nothing was working my doctor insisted on the IBS diagnosis when I went back week after week. Eventually I was given blood tests that showed infection, but nothing was done about it except repeat bloods every two weeks "to see if it goes away".

That was how I found myself in a hospital bed, trying not to cry as Mum finally went home at 2am to get some sleep.

The next day I had a scan that revealed two large cysts – 8cms on my right ovary and 5cms on my left ovary. My anatomy was a bit of a jigsaw puzzle, with my ovaries pushed up near my belly button and my womb near-invisible squashed between them. It was a surprise to say the least – I thought I'd just been getting fat!

After a few days on antibiotics to get the infections under control I had exploratory surgery to diagnose the cysts and drain them. It was at this point I was diagnosed with Stage IV Endometriosis – a condition where endometrial cells are found outside the womb, attached to the stomach lining and other organs. It was quite a shock, I can tell you that! It started what has been a 2 year journey of treatment, discoveries, education and healing that I'm still on to this day.

My cysts were so large that they couldn't remove them in the first surgery, so part of my treatment was 3 months on a drug called Zoladex, an implant in your stomach that induces a medical menopause, to shrink them. That experience was a whole story in itself! 4 months later I had my second surgery to remove the cysts and as much of the endometriosis as they could, along with checking my fertility.

When I came round from the anaesthetic my consultant explained they couldn't remove all of the endometriosis – my fallopian tubes were attached to my bowel, which they weren't able to separate. Plus the news we'd been dreading: my tubes were completely blocked, meaning my eggs couldn't get through. At this point there were a few tears before my body shut down. I couldn't cope – I've wanted to be a mother for as long as I can remember, even seeing myself as a second mum to my sister when I was just 2 years old – so I slept for the next 24 hours.

Once I was home it was time to heal in any way I could. I had a coil to slow the re-growth of Endo and I got even more focused on the Endo Diet (which you can read about on my blog). I lost a lot of weight in the early days and did everything I could to keep a positive mind-set, but I kept getting pulled back by the infertility. There were reminders everywhere – friends were having children, there were children on the bus, I had to walk through the 'little people' section in Ikea…

I was the woman crying in public at the sight of children and I hated it. My body was letting me down in every sense and it was a very rocky time in our household. Tom has been amazing and has done everything he can to help me from the first symptom through to today, but some things can't be healed by another person.

I breezed through the first half of 2014 thinking I was doing well – I started my own business that was very successful in the early days, most of my pain disappeared and (if you ignored the little people, which I was trying to) I was feeling better in myself.

The further into the year I got, the more I realised the impact of my experiences and illness. I was trying to heal and mask severe depression by putting a plaster on it. I was developing social anxiety as I was too scared my pain would flare up while I was out. My business wasn't doing so well, so I ended up spending more and more time home alone and feeling like I'd lost my sense of self.

All of my pre-Endo hobbies had disappeared, some because I didn't have the energy and others just because. I spent much of my time aimlessly online or watching TV shows to pass time. At this point I gave in once again and resigned myself to "this is it". I had an okay life – I went out now and then, I had an amazing family supporting me, I could live with that.

Remember how I said things change when you give in? Well, they do. For me sometimes it's in the most spectacular way possible (and not always in the good sense!). In March 2015 I was taken ill at work – vomiting and a fever that came on very suddenly. I assumed it was a 24 hour stomach bug, but after 5 days of no food and little water I slowly started turning yellow. Uh-oh…

I was admitted to hospital again and after 5 days, LOTS of antibiotics and 2 emergency surgeries I came home without a gallbladder to start the recovery process again. By this point I even doubted my abilities – could I ever have a 'normal' life? Would it just be one illness after another?

What should have been a 2 week recovery turned into a 2 month recovery and even now I'm not back to 100%. This time it's different though. Throughout all of this I've had a strong, stubborn streak that just wouldn't let me quit. I've given in to the help of others, I've given in to the universe, but I've never given up and it took me 2 years to see that.

Now instead of fighting to get 'back to me' I'm discovering who I am – with Endo, without a gallbladder – who is Ami in her current form? What does she like, what does she love? What makes her tired (housework, no joke intended!) and what energises her (spending time with family)? Possibly the scariest step – how will we bring a family of our own into this world? It will be another journey, but it's one we'll take on together.

If I've learned just one thing through all of this, it's that you've got to have your tribe. For some that's family, for others it's friends, but you can't make it through alone.

My family were my cheering squad, believing in me when I couldn't. They were my house elves, cleaning and cooking when I was good for nothing but sleep. They were my army when it was time to fight anyone who wasn't listening to my needs and they were shoulders on the hundreds of times I needed to cry on one. I lost myself in the journey, but they always knew I was in here and they've done everything possible and more to help me back out.

Whether you're going through health problems or just not being heard in your life, my advice is to advocate for yourself. Give in when you need to, but never, ever give up on yourself. Gather your tribe, make your plan of attack and then just **go for it**!

Brian Fakir

Brian Fakir is a qualified Electrical Engineer who went on to specialise in fire safety. He is also a Geology graduate. He has finally found his niche in the gourmet healthy coffee industry, doing the work he was born to do, known locally as the King of Coffee.

He is the author of a business book for small businesses and start ups and is a future novelist. He has a supportive wife, loves his children and grandchildren, and loves helping people realise their goals and dreams are there for the taking. It's not wrong to dream.

You can reach Brian at:

Website:
http://www.brianfakir.myorganogold.com/

Facebook:
https://www.facebook.com/brian.fakir.3

Twitter:
https://twitter.com/Im_KingofCoffee

I'm Not Going To Spend My Life Being A Colour
By Brian Fakir

What colour is success? People have always associated colour with some form of emotion. For example, that person has a sunny disposition indicating yellow for happiness or when the red mist forms indicating anger, and green with envy for jealousy. Is there a colour for success, is success an emotion? YOU might think that success equals desire; 'I desire success'. A desire is formed from an emotion, one that makes you smile, makes your heart beat faster, pushing adrenalin through your body, a bit like a roller coaster at a fun fair. So my question is what colour is success?

Born in a mixed race family, my mother is British and my father is North African. I was born in the 1950s; the seeds of racism had already been sown in America and were permeating the United Kingdom. If you've met me before in my adult life, you will ask 'What did all that have to do with you?' You will find how instrumental that part of my life was and how it shaped who I am today.

My parents, bless them, decided that both myself and my sister would escape racism by denomination. We weren't going to be Muslims; we would be Christians, Church of England baptists. What that didn't do was change my colour or my name.

Throughout my primary, yes would you believe primary school, all the way through secondary school, I endured both physical and verbal racist abuse. The effect that had on me was cataclysmic: my only thoughts were, "This is going to be my life forever." I became very shy, insular, nervous, a bed wetter because of my nerves and I lacked all confidence. Everything was always out of my reach because of the word can't. 'You can't do that' and 'You can't be what you want to be'.

As soon as I was able to read properly I found solace in books. The written word was my saviour. I found something I loved, yet the comments started to roll in. 'Always got his head in a book, that boy, why isn't he doing something for himself?' Authors didn't know who I was or pre-judge me. I was reading words without prejudice. I could lose myself in a world of detectives, sports stars and explorers. I could escape and forget my outside world in a book.

What about friends? Of course I had friends, whether I found them or they found me is unclear; however those friends are still here in my life today and wherever they may be in the world, there is always time for a hello through Social Media. Mostly they were from other mixed race families, not necessarily ethnic origin, but they were Israelis, Italians, Portuguese, Spanish, Russian and a smattering of British friends who didn't have any baggage or were taught that people should be liked whatever their origin.

In high school I was streamed into the higher levels of education because of my intelligence. It soon became evident that due to my own issues, my education path was taking a turn for the worse. I was put into the stream that needed help; a slow learner. This put me right into the hands of my persecutors. My parents would not intervene despite my protestations, unreservedly telling me that I had to fight my own battles. I went further and further into my own despair. I was a failure, academically and personally. How was this possible? I was well read, had great knowledge, but known as a failure. It was fear. Fear of asking questions and fear of rejection because I would be told 'Don't be so stupid' and I failed.

I did as I was told, did everything everyone wanted, got jobs I didn't want and everything else that went with it for the next 15 to 20 years. I fumbled and bumbled my way with no clear direction or guidance.

What about success then? I was, 'a successful failure', the only thing I could comfortably accomplish. That had to change. I read books and magazines, and they all ran adverts about becoming your own boss. I dreamt about it, and wouldn't dare tell anyone that my dream was to one day be my own boss. That is where it stayed. Being well read, I was good at something: research. I was about to change.

I changed my attitude for success. Initially I thought it was about being a boss, building a business, employing people, and making money. To a degree that is true, that is what most people want to do and most do it with degrees of success too. However that was still an unattainable dream for me in that moment. I had work to do first; I had to learn.

With every change I implemented, opportunity presented itself. Here were all the things I couldn't do previously because of the, 'You'll never be good enough' message I'd been given.

I applied to university and was immediately accepted as a mature student. What did I study and more to the point, what couldn't I study? There were no limits. I had a choice. Pandora's Box was now open and taking orders.

I majored in science and discovered subjects that interested me, mainly ones that didn't involve a career path because this was just about fuelling my drive and curiosity. I specialised in Biology, the shape of the Brain and Behaviour and Geology and rock shapes.

These two subjects were about to shape me. I qualified with a BSc, it took a long time balancing work and family life, but it was so worth it.

Work opportunities began to present themselves on their own. I was head hunted for almost every job I've had since. I still dreamt of being my own boss though and I tapped into the knowledgebase of these people I worked for. They saw something in me and I delivered. No longer did I have to hide behind my colour or blame it, I embraced it wholeheartedly.

I figured out how to handle people and make friends with them, how to be interested in them and get them interested in me. My world was turning inside out for the positive. I was bouncing back.

In 2000 my magic opportunity came. I was in a position with no commitments other than to myself and was offered an opportunity to start a business with a friend who I'd been encouraging to do this for months. We put our heart and soul into it, I brought all the things I'd learned from my previous mentors and we soared, always sticking to our roots of not being greedy. Things moved at a rapid pace and one part of the business moved faster than the other. I took the gamble and moved myself away and went solo. It was to be what I call 'divine intervention' because of bitterness another person took my friend's business away from him. He lost everything; home, family and friends.

I took on another business; I used everything I knew from before and continued to learn. I became a success, not financially necessarily, but with people. Unfortunately the economic climate took that business at its peak. People pulled their apron strings, as you would. But I knew I had the wherewithal not to give up.

Walking around Tesco one night, I bumped into my old business partner. We hadn't spoken properly for about three years and that's when he told me what happened. There and then an opportunity was realised. We met and talked for hours. The one thing he said has always stayed with me, 'We were friends first and we'll always be friends. Business is business, we might fall out, but that's where it stays'. He wanted my help and I needed him for my sanity.

In short, that's where we are today. I have used every opportunity that has come my way to springboard me to where I am now. I have friends around the world; I am respected for what I have to say. I'm a published author, I speak weekly to groups of people about what I do and they listen, to me, interested in what I have to say. I sell my products in five European countries.

I look back at my heroes in the books and comics I read and absorbed myself with; they all had superpowers and wore capes, could detect crime, and save the world. Now I see it as a bit more fundamental. All my heroes helped people and that is what I really wanted to do. It has now defined who I am and how I've bounced back. Just like the song by David Bowie, 'We can be heroes, if just for one day'.

'You must know that in any moment a decision you make can change the course of your life forever, the very next person you stand behind in line or sit next to on an airplane, the very next phone call you make or receive, the very next movie you see or book you read or page you turn could be the one single thing that causes the floodgates to open and all of the things you've been waiting for to fall into place'. - Courtesy of *Anthony Robbins*

Deb Hawken

Deb Hawken is an author, life coach, inspirational speaker and medium who helps people to heal their grief, find their truth and live their authentic life.

Deb always seeks the simplest solutions to help her clients create change and her first book "Who am I, Where am I, What is this Place?" offers straightforward ideas to help readers create change as quickly and easily as possible.

Deb follows a path of practical spirituality that has helped her change her life completely. She now uses all her training to help her clients do the same.

Book available from Amazon, Barnes & Noble, Waterstones (online), Google Play Books; signed copies by emailing Deb at deb@debhawken.com.

You can reach Deb at:

Website:
www.debhawken.com

Email:

deb@debhawken.com

Facebook:

https://www.facebook.com/DebHawkenTransformationalExpert
https://www.facebook.com/debhawkenwriter

Twitter:

https://twitter.com/debdancingstar

Is Your Bounce Weighed Down By Your Past?
By Deb Hawken

You can't lose your past so you may as well use your past.

A huge element of the need to change your life is firmly in your past. Whether it has been one of deep hurt, like mine, or whether you feel that you've made a number of wrong decisions leading to the wrong destination, popular thinking decrees that the past is something that must be let go of or forgotten in order to heal and move on; easier said than done.

I've worked in the counselling and spiritual fields for many years and lost count of the times I've heard people blithely say, "You have to let go of the past" or "just forget the past". Both lovely ideas and both practically impossible to achieve.

The mythical 'letting go' and the impossible 'forgetting' can stall our thinking and create barriers to change. The inability to let go or forget can also make us feel stupid. That wretched idiot who can't stop thinking or talking about their past! If you see that person coming fake illness and run!

However, there is a way that I personally have found very useful in helping me deal with and move on from my past: negativity! A scary idea? Maybe, but let's try it. Let's fully dive into the negativity of this situation and discover our bounce at the bottom of it. I promise that we will come up with arms full of roses in about 1300 more words.

Let's begin with letting go. To me the idea is mythical because I can't get hold of anything to let go of. A random thought will lurch into my mind, upset my digestion and disappear back into its hiding place before I can grab the little lurker and throttle it.

How do you let go of memories? What is it you let go of? We can all understand letting go of a hand or a rope, but we are being asked to perform a physical 'letting go' action of something that only exists in our minds. That isn't going to work.

As for forgetting, this is where I will be very blunt. In order to forget your past, you will need a serious brain illness or head injury. It's as factual as that; there is no other way to forget the past, so perhaps you might feel comforted by the idea that you don't really want to forget the past.

Factually speaking, the past is always in there somewhere and when something happens in the present that reminds us of the past the memories will surface. It's the way the human mind is built; the trouble is it doesn't have a selective off switch.

Think about this for a moment: if you went to someone's wedding and were reminded of your own would that be a bad thing? (Okay it might, but work with me here!) If a baby is born and you are reminded of your own bundles of joy and some of the greatest moments of your life, is that a bad thing? Of course not and no one will criticise you for remembering.

Yet it's a different story when you are put in a situation where something horrible is triggered. Family and friends might sigh and mutter "For goodness sake let it go", and make you feel stupid. Counsellors may ask you how that makes you feel and you dare not say "Crap, I told you that last time!" Coaches may tell you that you need to move past this and create a new future and you know that, but may not know how.

For me the idea of not having memories triggered by the past would require us to use the same mind in two different ways and the memory works in only one way so we have to take the rough with the smooth. Just as there is no blame attached to having a good memory pop up, there is no blame in having a bad memory do the same. One of the best ways to heal your life is to accept that as a fact.

Now we have 814 words left in order to find those roses.

Just as you put manure on roses to make them grow, you can use the manure of your past as fertiliser for a brilliant future. Instead of trying to forget the past think of it as a tool forged in a furnace that has the strength of steel. Every single hurt, disappointment and heartache can be used as fuel for a great future.

I don't talk about my past often because I don't need to. It's all still there, I haven't forgotten (thank God) and I haven't let it go. What I have done is to change myself and my life in such a way that the reminders of the past rarely pop up, because:

I no longer live the kind of life that gives them the opportunity.

In the past 20 years I have achieved more than I ever dreamed possible:

- Discovered spiritual thinking

- Divorced my first husband

- Married my soul mate - yes we do fight; no it doesn't matter

- Earned 2 degrees and a black belt

- Gained qualifications in Counselling and Life Coaching

- Mostly conquered acute anxiety; totally conquered fear of flying

- Had articles published in several spiritual magazines

- Presented a radio show with Nicky Marshall

- Written and produced a play and a musical

- Been on the television (for less than 15 minutes)

- Became a working Medium and inspirational speaker

- I travel internationally with my work, and on holiday

This from a person who suffered from crippling anxiety and still doesn't know how she kept going for over 30 years of complete misery, loneliness, criticism, ridicule, unfairness, spite, betrayal, bullying, being constantly wrong, and completely unimportant.

When asked how many children my parents had, my mother would always answer "Three, Peter, Neil and Debbie." Peter was my ex and my brother was younger than me, yet I always came third. As Tony once pointed out when I said I was afraid to try things "That's because your family ruined every good moment of your life" and then he explained what he as an outsider had seen.

My father once said that the worst thing he could say about anyone was that they wanted to be their best. I asked did he mean be better than others. To which he replied "No, just be their best, that's arrogance and showing off." Now you know why I'm amazed that I ever achieved anything.

I can't go into my life story any further as it takes thousands of words and hours of misery to write it and of course rehashing it would trigger those memories I don't want to forget. However, the achievements listed are only the major milestones; there have been millions more small achievements and wonderful moments.

I still have my challenges but I'm no longer frightened, sad, lonely and exhausted all the time. I achieved that by facing my negative past head on and I triumphed over it by using every hurt as a tool for positive change.

I survived and thrived by creating a new me and building my confidence based on reality. I now know who I am and what I can do. I also know who I'm not and what I can't do - and I'm fine with that, I'm human after all. Gloriously, magnificently human! Like you.

Reality is critical to a happy life and discovering your bounce. People might talk about faking it until you make it but I never fake it. If there's something I can't do I will tell you and if it matters to me I will go out and change that. My confidence is such that I have no need to pretend to you and I don't need to apologise for being a human and therefore fallible being (only for my mistakes).

Pretending does not represent true healing, that just plays into the hands of the past in a big way, and believe me, life will test you and your carefully constructed persona will come crashing down like a house of cards in the first slight breeze.

There are over 7 billion people on this planet and not one is perfect.

Be fearlessly human - everyone else is no matter what masks they wear or philosophies they invoke and no one needs apologise for getting something wrong, feeling weak and vulnerable, or failing to cope.

We all have such times and the most important thing is to acknowledge them. If you can accept your own truth and work with it, rather than hide from it and pretend it doesn't exist, you will win. You will change. You will take control of your life. You will feel better. Like me, you will experience real miracles.

All of this has happened because of my past.

Every single good thing that has happened in the last 30 years has happened because I've used all of my past as fuel for positive change and you can do this too. The past is a lesson that learned well and used properly will create a fantastic future.

This brings me to my final point. The form of spirituality I follow and teach, is a practical method of living your life in the real world. Briefly, it relies on you discovering the aspect of your being that we are not taught to seek - your true spiritual or higher self. This might sound far-fetched or complex, you may have no idea where to look, how to look or what to look for, but it can be done and here's how.

Your true being will be revealed by facing and living your truth.

That's how you discover your bounce!

Emma-Joel Coker

Once upon a time there was a little girl named Emma-Joel Coker, who amongst all the madness and chaos of her childhood found an amazing sense of freedom in reading her favourite books. Emma-Joel's dream was to one day become a famous Author and pen her own fiction novel based upon her extraordinary upbringing.

That dream has now taken flight. To date, I have spent 20 years working with individuals across the globe to attract and coach talented, well beings. My holistic approach enables individuals and companies to work from a mind, body and spirited way in their everyday working lives. I assist clients to achieve personal and professional goals that are not born out of stress.

I have a first class degree in life and a passion for excellence when it comes to seeing my clients find their wings and soar to the heights they set themselves. Life is too short to not live it in a passionate and compelling fashion because even though a storm may arise there will ultimately be a rainbow.

You can reach Emma, The Holistic Head Hunter at:

Email:
Emma@theholisticheadhunter.com

Facebook:
www.facebook.com/TheHolisticHeadhunter

Website:
www.theholisticheadhunter.com

Twitter:
https://twitter.com/HolisticHH

47 Minutes
By Emma-Joel Coker

I looked at the clock and pronounced the time just like you hear them do in the movies. Time of death 9:51am. I sat there motionless, glued to the spot, but calm for the first time in days.

Nobody prepares you for this moment so you do what you think is best, is expected, or you feel is what any dying person might want. Nobody prepares you for the death of your father and nobody prepares you for the death of your father when you are sitting in bed right next to him.

I closed his eyes, stroked his forehead, and sat there staring at the clock. I had given myself 9 minutes before I would call the nurse, I wanted those last precious minutes of just me and him before the process started where he would be in the hands of "others" or hospital staff as they were really known. Over a period of months and weeks they had become well known to me, but on this occasion they were strangers and I didn't want them anywhere near me for those last few precious minutes.

I don't suppose any child has a plan when their parent dies, but in our heads we sort of know it's going to hurt, we know it's going to come and we do our best not to discuss it, well especially not with "them". I sadly am a bit different. I did have a plan, I did sort of know what I would do and we had sort of discussed it.

My Father was an alcoholic, there you go, I've said it…God rest his soul! It's taken years for me to say that and even now I can see my Dad looking away from me and shaking his head. In fact, I can almost hear him tutting! He wasn't your standard alcoholic, he didn't drink blue cans of tenants extra, dress like a tramp or live in squalor. He was well groomed, his home was his castle and his car was so clean you could literally eat your dinner off it. My father was very hard-working, travelled the globe and was a one-off in his field of work. In fact, just before he passed away he was one of only five people schooled and experienced in a certain make of generator and companies paid a lot of money to contract my Father for that knowledge. Hence the reason his tipple was champagne, his favourite meal was lobster and before he died he bought a Bentley, which he proudly drove to the launderette.

We had a troubled relationship. We went months, sometimes years between speaking and seeing each other and at times I wished he wasn't my father. Some people said we were too alike, some people said we looked alike, but for many years all I felt was shame. I felt shame for all the times we argued, for the fear I had and for all the times we missed.

Luckily for me he never gave up and luckily for him neither did I. You see I loved him; I loved him so deeply I thought my heart might burst. When we did get the chance for a hug he held me so tightly I could literally feel all the broken pieces fitting back together and I felt safe. I can remember those hugs as if they were only yesterday.

They said on arrival to A&E that I was a day too early, that they had not got all the tests back yet and could I not come back tomorrow. I was in Bruges, we had come by Taxi and my father was literally dying in front of me. The cancer had really taken hold over the last few weeks and his bones were beginning to break, he weighed 54 kilos and he couldn't swallow anymore because the tumours were so large. The doctor said they suspected TB and I laughed. I didn't mean to laugh, but really could they not just deal with the obvious and stop trying to be so clever. I did my best not to shout and handed them the doctor's note. I didn't speak the language so I had asked my father's doctor to explain why I had hailed a cab from Holland to Brugge. Thankfully the letter did the job.

I whispered in my dad's ear, "They think you have TB." He grinned as if to say 'oh good it's not cancer' and I smiled. He really didn't want to die of something so obvious.

I had always envisaged a phone call, a lady who I hadn't met, but with bright red nails and a hand full of expensive rings calling me to say that he was dead. I imagined a trip to his house where I had never been to collect a load of bin bags, a few pictures and maybe the odd strange item like a sword or a diving knife. I certainly didn't imagine climbing into bed next to him, putting my arms around him and saying goodbye from everyone in my family. I didn't imagine telling him I was going to be great, ok, fine and all would be well as he gasped his last breath and I certainly didn't think it would be 1 mile up the road from where his parents were killed. I didn't imagine it would take 47 minutes!

At exactly 10am I took a deep breath, untangled my hand from my father's now very cool grip and walked towards the door. It had been chaos on floor 11 of the hospital before my father passed, but now all I could feel was silence, an eerie void, as if the whole world had been put in slow motion. The attending nurse appeared, took my hand and cried. In fact several nurses appeared, gave me a hug, consoled me in broken English and Dutch and then stood to one side as I was motioned along the corridor to the nurse's station. I glanced behind me one more time to my father's room, I knew what needed to happen next and I was given a 30 minute break whilst they "laid him to rest" in a hospital fashion and filled out a few forms. I had been asked to select some clothes that I might like him to be dressed in upon my return, but alas I hadn't packed very well. I hadn't really given much thought to what I might like my father to wear. Dear God he loved clothes and shoes, but today was not going to be his proudest moment of fashion. It troubled me and I began to feel the tears pour down my cheeks. How could something so silly start me off? How could something so meaningless after all that I had experienced in that room bring me to my knees in the hospital canteen? But it did!

I proceeded to let the tears stream down my face and was now void of expression and words. I could feel all eyes upon me as I continued to be amongst "The Dutch". You see, I was now all alone, orphaned and in unfamiliar territory with absolutely no clue as to what I should, could or would do next. Who should I call, who really cares and who really wants to know? What the hell do I say? Regrettably my mother and father had parted badly when I was very young, my sister and I had different fathers and I was now divorced. Who in God's name can I tell? 30 seconds later a name appeared in my head. It was Joery, the son my father never really had, but I knew he meant the world to him. I had only met him once when he was 9, but Joery was now 24 and we were about to meet for the second time and in a very different setting. One where at least he could survive. He was born in Holland, a native, spoke several languages and was about to become the only family member in my life who could even understand or share my pain. I was grateful.

I was asked to return to "The Room" for one last time to greet my father and to say goodbye. He was now stiff with an odd looking smirk on his face that was a result of his last gasp. I wondered if it was because all I had to dress him in was a t-shirt with a logo of 'The Jam' on it, a pair of blue and white check summer trousers and a cravat. I still to this day think that is exactly what his smirk was about. It helps me to think he might have been smiling behind that exterior pose he now gave.

I felt empty, sick, dazed and in a great amount of indescribable emotional pain. I kissed his forehead, gazed into his beautiful blue eyes and held his hand for the last time.

However 3 years on I am eternally grateful. I wouldn't have had it any other way and although it hurt like hell and still does, it has been one of my richer experiences. From that moment, nothing in my life has ever been the same and never will be.

My father left me a gift, in fact he left me many gifts, but the one I value the most is his legacy of writing. He wrote pages and I found them all. He loved life, he liked it fast and he liked it hard and now it's my turn to tell our story.

Freyja P. Jensen

Freyja is an effervescent, polished Human Resources Recruitment and Networking Professional, Relationship Manager, Recruitment Consultant and Coach, Public Speaker, Office Administrator and Executive Ninja as well as a Mother, an Oma, a Daughter, Sister and valued Friend. She believes our voices matter and that it's important to stand up and be heard. Her mission is to speak as an advocate on behalf of those who have yet to find their voices by bravely and openly sharing personal experiences and growth via Networking, Media, and PR opportunities. Freyja is a published writer and a two time International Best-selling Author.

You can reach Freyja P. Jensen at:

Email:
fpjays@live.ca
Freyja.Jensen@OpenForChange.com

LinkedIn:
www.linkedin.com/in/executiveninja

Twitter:
www.twitter.com/fpjays

Facebook:
www.facebook.com/norse.viking.goddess

There Is No Ordinary In Extraordinary
By Freyja P. Jensen

I never thought that recovery from an illness or a traumatic experience would be so genuinely empowering, but through my adversity – through the changes and experiences, I have become a brave, fierce, courageous Viking Warrior Goddess. I am an advocate now for those who are afraid to use their voices to fight to overcome or defend themselves. It has not always been that way.

As part of my original chapter in the first book I contributed to, Inch By Inch: Growing In Life, I wrote about overcoming adversity as a child. From being traumatized by witnessing my Mother's death while she was mutilated in a horrific train crash in front of my eyes, to being subjected to molestation, degradation, humiliation, and then rape and because what happened behind closed doors stayed there, there was no outlet for safety. Being bullied by my peers, parents, siblings, school mates, being made to feel insignificant, worthless and useless, scraped whatever self-worth I was born with right off the grid of this innocent child's life.

In the next book I joined as a co-author, The Missing Piece in Forgiveness, I wrote about how I overcame the experiences that shaped me into who I became and how through my spiritual path, because of my faith, I was able to forgive those who had hurt me and took my childhood from me.

In the last ten years, I have finally grasped and accepted that I live with mental illness, which is in fact a condition that impacts a person's thinking, feeling or mood, and may affect his or her ability to relate to others and function on a daily basis. Admitting to having a mental illness was one of the hardest things I ever had to come to terms with because copping to it meant that I was weak and broken. I learned early on which masks to wear in order to survive.

I remember one night when my son was about 3 years old and would not stop crying. I was so frustrated and overwhelmed. As a single Mom struggling, going to school, working two part-time jobs, and trying to make ends meet to provide for my child, I was suddenly at my wit's end. I reacted with the same yelling, angry tone that my father had used with me. The moment I realized what I was doing, that I sounded like my father, I fell to my knees in tears beside my son and just held him. I was so sorry and so sad that I had reacted poorly that I could only say to him that this was not his fault, but that his Mommy was hurting and the anger was not meant for him. It was towards myself. I was ashamed. It was time for help to come – somehow, some way, it always came. I prayed.

It was a weekend Personal Best seminar that I was invited to shortly after the experience with my son that would change the direction of my life. I remember how illuminating it was to me and how it felt like an awakening of Freyja. I remember one particular exercise in which we had been individually chosen to be lifted up by our group, candles lit around the room, when a song began to play. My cradle song they called it, chosen specifically for me. Being lifted up, trusting all of those around me that I had shared my most intimate secrets and pain with to keep me safe and protected, was a feeling of re-birth. The music played, "You Are So Beautiful To Me" by Joe Cocker. For the first time since I could remember, at 28 years old, I felt beautiful and worthy of love. I had bounced back from a hell I had grown up to know to realizing I had value.

It took many more turns in my life, which included 3 marriages and several relationships where I tried to get it right. Once I had realized my worth, my self-esteem grew, but my confidence wavered and the school of life, of hard-knocks kept testing me. I wanted a healthy relationship, one that would nurture me, provide the love I needed so desperately and also bring a good role-model and male influence into my son's life. What I realized following my 3rd marriage is that to have a healthy relationship, one needs to know what healthy is. I had no memory of what that should look like from my parents. It was through life-long learning, countless counsellors and workshops, groups and reading on the subject of healing for me to find the love I felt I needed. What I did not grasp until more recently is that in order to be loved, we must learn to love ourselves.

That path my friends, was one bounce after another... continuously growing, getting knocked down and then climbing back up again. I went from being the victim to being gloriously victorious. The experiences were countless; good and bad. I never gave up. Having my son in my life, even after he had left home, gave me purpose to survive.

Just when I thought the worst was over, I was faced with a whole new life shift in the last 10 years. My path changed again. I realized through some further horrific experiences that people could be incredibly cruel and that they were not just from my childhood, but those that I worked, lived, and played with as adults. I was tormented by people who suffered from their own addictions. I came face to face with the realization that I was not alone with mental illness. I have since learned that genetics, environment, and lifestyle combine to influence whether someone develops a mental health condition. A stressful job or home life makes some more susceptible than others, as do traumatic life events.

With a previous employer, I experienced adult bullying, which landed me in the hospital with a partial stroke. It was a wake-up call for help. It was time to admit that I indeed had a serious illness and I needed to face it.

I've been diagnosed with PTSD, depression, anxiety and panic disorder, adrenal fatigue, IBS and a plethora of digestive issues, ADHD, and ADSD. Most people who know me would never consider that I also have OCD, agoraphobia, and social phobia, as on the outside I am an incredibly outgoing, vivacious, effervescent, well-put together social diva. I have in fact cancelled appointments and commitments because I could not face them for many reasons. I could go through a depressive state where I would hide in a closet and just cry my eyes out feeling worthless and having suicidal thoughts. I remember my father saying to me that I would never amount to anything because I was too stupid. Every once in a while, that nasty dragon rears its fiery head to test and taunt me.

My saving grace is that now I reach out for help when I need it, I take medication to keep me level and surround myself with positive and encouraging people. I live a life in which I try and see the good in everyone and treat them as I wish to be treated. Admitting I am flawed makes me real and that makes me relatable and approachable and I am grateful for being blessed with an enormous amount of courage and most of all – love. I realize that I am not alone and if you are reading this now and can relate in any way, you are also not alone. There is help out there. Reach for it. It is important that you know that this is all treatable and you don't have to live an ordinary life, but are worthy of living an extraordinary life. I am worth it and so are you. Change can be chaotic, messy and sometimes scary and perhaps like you, there are times when I just want to run in the other direction. Being introspective forces me to be incredibly honest with my own life and reach out beyond my comfort zone for the help I need.

Every day I do my best to lead a positive, productive life and what is most rewarding to me is when I can be an advocate for those who are having difficulties finding their voices. My desire is to leave a legacy of love which is about putting love into action and sustaining it for a better world by making the world a better place to live in. I have good and bad days, but one thing remains strong and steadfast; my passion for life, love, family, friends, people, and my undeniable will to live authentically and with purpose.

Thich Nhat Hanh says, "Sit down and take an inventory of your life. If there are things you have been hanging on to that are not useful and deprive you of your freedom, find the courage to let them go. An overloaded boat is easily capsized by wind and waves. Lighten your load and your boat will travel more quickly and safely. Then you can offer the precious gift of freedom and space to yourself and loved ones, but only if it is truly there in your heart."

Never give up - bounce back and remember – there is no ordinary in extraordinary and you are extraordinary!

Rainbows, hearts, love, and blessings to you all.

Freyja P. Jensen

Hali Jafari

Hali will help you choose a healthier approach to eating and introduce you to delicious foods that help to nourish your body with her recipe blog and lifestyle coaching.

Hali was overweight for 20 years, using food as comfort to get her through life after suffering abuse at a young age. Learning to overcome her food addiction has been a big challenge.

Hali shares with you how she took steps to change her life and step out of her comfort zone. Losing half her body weight has been a journey that has brought more than just a smaller dress size.

You can reach Hali at:

Website:
www.trulynourished.co.uk

Twitter:
@TNourished

Facebook:
www.facebook.com/TNourished

Instagram:
<u>Truly Nourished</u>

Survival Of The Nourished
By Hali Jafari

Running as fast as I could with his voice in my ears, "I know your dad, so you better not tell him what a disgusting little girl you are!"

All I could think was, 'Please don't tell my dad!'

I felt embarrassed, how could I be so stupid?! I ran as fast as I could down the alleyway that led to my home with my heart beating so fast in my little body. I saw my grandma at the front door and I breathed a sigh of relief, yet worry crossed my mind as I wondered if she could tell what had happened and if she thought I'd been a bad girl.

That was 23 years ago. I was a 9 year old girl who got stopped by a poor old blind man. He asked me for directions to an address. I was naive and kind and I took him to the house he was asking directions for. I didn't know he was lying, I didn't know he was going to pull my collar, touch my childlike body and hold on to me violently whilst he got out his keys and opened his front door. Those seconds before I found the strength to kick him in the balls, push past and run from him felt like hours.

That was the day my relationship with myself disintegrated. It was the day I ran home and hid in the wardrobe with a cake and a milkshake and shoved it down my throat so fast I could barely taste it. It was the day I learned how to hate every inch of my body.

49

Unfortunately for me this wasn't a one-off incident. Worse was to come and my secret eating became more frequent and my weight crept up month by month, year by year. Without going into specifics, I then endured sexual abuse on a daily basis for a whole year of my life, whilst on my way to school every morning. I became ashamed of myself and frightened of people.

My bad relationship with food continued through my teenage years and into my adulthood, as did my poor self-esteem, which sank lower and lower. The vicious cycle had started and the more I ate - the more I hated myself - and so the more I ate!

This habit formed so deep inside me that I knew no other way; food was my medicine, my drug and my comfort. Over-eating, bingeing, starving and self-hatred became the norm for me and I had well and truly blocked out and forgotten about the abuse. In fact, it wasn't until 15 years after, during a debilitating bout of postnatal depression after giving birth to my daughter that I began to have flashbacks and it all came flooding back.

For years I focused on the past and the pain it caused and in January 2013 I had a nervous breakdown.

The years I spent blocking out the past, living in denial about my weight and hating myself had taken its toll. One day I just couldn't get out of bed. I wasn't physically stuck to my bed, but mentally I could not face another day. I stayed in bed for 3 months, unable to function, not wanting to see or talk to anyone and suffered panic attacks on a regular basis. Even trying to think of making a meal for my children was impossible. The depression had set in hard and made me question so much about my life and the choices I had made up until that point in my life. I realised how I had been using my body fat as armour and protection. It was my comfort blanket that I could use as an excuse to avoid doing the things I wanted to do in life but was scared to. I could be fat and unattractive to protect myself from people and situations that made me feel so uncomfortable.

From January until March 2013, I couldn't work or sleep. I even stopped eating as much, which was strange for me! I went from 22 stone (308lbs), to 20 stone 10lbs (290lbs) without even trying. I was ill, mentally and physically exhausted. I slept for most of the day while staying awake for hours at night with thoughts whizzing round my head and I began to have suicidal thoughts that scared me.

I had counselling and my antidepressants were increased to a maximum dose. My doctor saw me every week and slowly I began to see more reasons to live. The flowers blooming as spring arrived, the Easter holidays coming up, even the simple things such as the sunset became beautiful again. Finding beauty in life again was difficult, but as time passed I realised I could get through this dark phase.

I began to reassess everything in my life. What was my purpose? What were my hopes? My dreams? Did I even know? This was when I realised that for as long as I allowed my past to control me, I would never know my purpose or my self-worth. And so it began, my 2 year journey of how I got to be here today. To be writing a piece for you to read and to be told that I'm an inspiration to others! Here's what I did...

I had 150lbs of excess weight to shift! I was morbidly obese with the cholesterol level of a 70 year old and I wasn't even 30 years old! I chose weight loss surgery as a way to help me shift this weight. Before you dismiss me as a cheat, believe me it wasn't easy and even now two years later, it's still not easy. I learned how to eat less and had to make healthier food choices every day. I knew I would never eat a huge Christmas dinner again or be able to have a weekend takeout or a binge drinking session ever again, but I didn't care, this weight had to go! The weight came off nice and steady and as time went by I began to feel healthier, I looked better, I was more relaxed and began to recognise something shift inside me. I find it hard to put into words the exact emotions I felt, I think the nearest word to describe what was happening was 'contentment'.

It took me just over 18 months to reach my target weight of 11 stone (154lbs) and I have kept it off for 6 months now. The two year journey that started as a way to get rid of past emotions became a rollercoaster with as many highs as it had lows. My weight loss became a subject that everyone wanted to talk to me about and I was more than happy to tell people why and how I'd done it. I was so proud of what I'd achieved and I knew how desperate they were feeling, I'd felt it myself throughout 20 years of failed dieting.

I went on to study and become a qualified Weight Loss Practitioner and I decided to start a blog called 'Truly Nourished', about my experience, as well as writing healthy recipes for people to follow. I'm currently working with a group of clients on my 14 Day Detox Plan. It's not just about detoxing from food, but rather unhealthy habits and beliefs too. I'm a firm believer in self-development. Life can continuously throw obstacles at us, challenging us sometimes beyond belief, but it's about becoming a better, happier and healthier version of yourself. Someone you can be proud of, rather than attempting another diet that will leave you feeling worthless and a failure! Being Truly Nourished is a job from within which you need to work on every day.

Since my weight loss, I have done many things I had never attempted before. I went swimming on my own for the first time in my life, I took my 3 children to a theme park and went on every single ride just because I could fit in all the seats and on the aeroplane I didn't need an extender belt! I have travelled alone around other cities for shows and work and not only did I love the feeling of freedom as opposed to being fearful of getting lost, but I also found out that I love to travel and I never knew this about myself! It's easy to label yourself as a homebody when you don't realise it's just fear that's stopping you from exploring.

Last month I was a winning contestant on a new cookery show hosted by one of my favourite chefs James Martin. Whilst I was cooking my dish on the show, I suddenly had a moment of thought, 'Here I am with cameras in my face, competing to win a cookery show in an unfamiliar kitchen with people I have never met before and just two years ago I couldn't go to the supermarket due to the anxiety it caused!'

I have put myself forward for so many opportunities this year and I feel unstoppable with the knowledge that I am the only one who can achieve higher and better every day by the choices I make. For me shedding my excess body weight was the secret to bouncing back, what's your barrier that's stopping you?

Helen Sanders

Helen Sanders is Leo's mum.

And when she's not being referred to as 'Leo's mum', she does try to carve out time for other things also!

She is a successful entrepreneur who thrives by helping expanding companies hire the right staff. Helen is also passionate about coaching those looking for a new job. She gets a real kick out of writing CVs that are successful in getting people an interview.

Helen has a varied background having previously had a successful career as a broadcaster, producer and assistant for the BBC in the UK as well as independent radio stations in the UK and US.

You can contact Helen at:

LinkedIn:
https://uk.linkedin.com/in/helenwingrovesanders

Live And Let Live
By Helen Sanders

Is he going to die?

Please don't tell me he's going to die.

The doctor said that she didn't know.

We were in the smallest office in the hospital. It was more like a cupboard. No windows. Tiny desk. And the smallest area for the doctor and I to sit next to each other.

The walls were inching closer and closer. A little like in Star Wars when Princess Leia along with Han Solo are in that crusher. Remember that? Well in my crusher, I was staring at a picture of my son's head on a PC screen. An MRI picture of his brain.

This brain didn't look right.

It didn't take a doctor to tell me that.

There was a huge white circle. It was in my son's brain.

This golf ball-sized tumour was pushing his right eyeball out of his head. It had eaten away some of the eye socket. What eats bone?

He was 3. How on earth can this doctor be telling me my only son had cancer?

I returned back to the hospital room where our son was so the doctor could then speak with my husband, our son's father. When I say returned to our son's bedside, I shuffled back. I don't normally walk without lifting my feet, but I was recovering from major surgery 5 days previously.

As a result of that surgery, my son, this son who now had cancer, was my only child and would be my only child. I can't have any brothers or sisters for him, but that's the least of our worries now.

It now feels like all this happened in a different time and place. Yes, it happened to our son. It certainly happened to our family and friends who did all they could to help us all, but it does feel like a very long time ago and not just 7 years ago.

He is alive. I'd like to say alive and well but essentially, when you blast radiotherapy at a child's brain at the age of 3, well, it's safe to say there's going to be some collateral damage.

Doctors repeatedly warn you. If your son survives, this, this and this will all happen. At the time, you only take on board what you need to be able to function and get through the next hour, day, perhaps the next week. Yes, my husband and I signed all the consent forms. We had to. No real choice. Your son needs to have poisons pumped through him which modern medicine calls chemotherapy and we must also blast lasers through his skull, into the tumour and out the other side of his brain.

Yes, we are not surprised by what doctors call late effects as they did tell us over and over again. Cataracts, no growth hormone, learning disabilities, early or late puberty, increase in secondary cancers, increased risk of skin cancer, cancer will return if he drinks or smokes and many other life altering things.

That is what these are. They're life altering. We do what we need to, in order to embrace the life-altering aspects of the past, bounce back as it were and create a new life. With purpose. A life which means as a result of the crap thrown at our son, we enable him to move past it, treat it for what it is. It was a horrid time in his life which wholly altered his path. You make new plans.

He would have died.

He didn't.

He is alive.

We live together, happily trying to ensure the cancer doesn't have the hold on us as it did back in 2008.

It altered our lives, but we are alive.

We, therefore, owe it to those families we met along the way who were taken into a similar cupboard of a room. We owe it to those children who fought with dignity and a smile most of the time, to ensure we live life with purpose.

I'm not saying that it always felt like this.

I will be honest.

The January after our son finished treatment, my husband wanted to go back to work. Treatment had finished in November. Weekly community nurse visits and hospital trips were all in hand, the central line had been removed and we'd also managed a few days in Disneyland Paris.

My husband wanted to return to work and I just didn't get it. I was fuming that he didn't want to spend every waking day with our son.

What if today was the day the cancer came back? What if his oncologist calls today and says he'd like to see us ASAP? Yet my husband's at work being 'normal'?

For two years, this is how the cancer controlled my head. It was in my brain. Not literally, but I could not get past what had happened to our son. It totally and utterly controlled my every cell. The cancer was still in our lives.

I am not too sure what happened, but I realised my husband was living life. I was so peeved at him for being 'normal' and carrying on.

It wasn't the life he had chosen or mapped out. No one thinks about what will happen after their son has cancer.

Similarly, our son was just living life too. He was only 4 and 5 during those two years post-treatment and he was giggling, playing, just being a child, albeit a child starting to struggle due to late effects.

It didn't quite go like that for me; I made sure our son slept with me every night. Yes, he wasn't sleeping well and yes, he had many nightmares about being the last person on the planet when we were all destroyed by volcanoes.

I wanted to sleep with our son by my side so that I could ensure that each time I woke up, I could check if he was still alive.

Was he still breathing?

Were his cute little hands still warm?

Thankfully each time it was yes to both questions. When I say each time, I think we're talking maybe ten to twenty times a night that I'd wake up to check he was still with us.

Somehow as the days, weeks and months went by, my brain was ridding itself of this control. Of the cancer.

I perhaps woke 5 times a night instead. This reduced to once or twice.

Then our son went into his own room and my husband and I returned to our own bed, together.

I began, very slowly, to realise that maybe we will be the lucky ones. We may just be the ones whose son survives. Some children do survive so perhaps our son is the one? Luck may be helping us here. Just as each day this small hint of a thought that luck was on our side grew bit by bit and the guilt subsided ever so slightly, I started to realise that I had a tremendous choice.

I could:

Live life. A new life.

Or live life suffocated by cancer.

Or mourn the life we had.

Or ….

The final 'or' does not warrant discussing.

The choice was obvious. I had to live life. The new life. Didn't I?

I owed it to the families and children who had also been told that their child had cancer. Plus the cancer may still return so what was I doing letting it control me so much?

I had to grab life by the scruff of the neck, stop being so pissed off with everyone for having 'normal' lives and move on.

We had another chance.

We had a new life. I just had to live it. The other options available were not options. Not really.

My husband had to return to work so quickly in order for him to cope with the new life we were now living. I now get that. It took me a whole two years. I am thankful for the opportunity to now be able to mould my life. That life means I can use our experience to ensure our son lives life well and with purpose.

Thoughts then were 'he can't die'. My thoughts now are he must live, live life well, and with purpose. Otherwise all this heartache, all the tears, all the stress to him, my husband and I, his grandparents, aunts and uncles and everyone around us who supported us, their stress (and the chemo and radiotherapy and blood transfusions and general anaesthetics and bone scans and the MRIs and everything else), it would have been pointless. If you're going to live, you may as well do it with purpose.

The doctor told me she wasn't sure if he was going to die.

Writing this now makes me think why I asked if he was going to die.

The 'me' of today would ask if he is going to live.

Same question.

But different phrase. Different outcome. Mightily different focus.

Joanna Coull

Joanna Coull is one of the UK's leading lifestyle financial planners.

Leaving university she embarked upon a career in financial services where she immediately discovered a talent for helping people take control of their finances.

Her passion for lifestyle financial planning is as strong today as it was when she started her career 30 years ago.

Always full of entrepreneurial spirit, in 2007 Joanna bought a pub and transformed it into an award winning business.

Unfortunately the recession got the better of her and the past two years have been dominated by incredibly dark moments. But she has battled back.

You can reach at Joanna at:

Website:
www.coullmoney.com

Email:
joanna@coullmoney.com
Facebook:

https://www.facebook.com/joanna.coull.3

LinkedIn:
https://uk.linkedin.com/pub/joanna-coull/42/174/a70

Against All Odds
By Joanna Coull

This is the epic tale of a one woman battle against the world's worst recession. A battle fought in a country pub that nestled in the idyllic Worcestershire countryside.

My story starts way back in 1984 when after graduating I became a financial adviser, much to the horror of friends and family. To their amazement, and mine, I actually demonstrated an instant flair and instinct for it. I discovered a love of communicating with people and a real enthusiasm for sorting out their financial challenges.

The wonderful part of being a good and passionate adviser is that through helping people achieve financial peace of mind it is possible to earn well and I did.

I married young at age 23. While my husband, a renowned violinist, followed his dream to perform around the world, I built a dream lifestyle for us both.

It involved fast cars and the house of my childhood dreams. A stunning converted barn in Warwickshire with acres of land where I could keep my horses and see them every morning when I got up and gazed out of my bedroom window.

The sad thing though, and I only realise it when I look back, is that I was lonely. I would spend hours, sometimes days, on my own. I know now I am a hugely sociable person not destined to be a loner.

Mid-life crisis came at age 45 when I decided to buy a country pub. An obvious choice to me, but again not to friends and family.

The buying of a pub was never going to be an easy process, but one of my strengths is resourcefulness and a determination not to be defeated.

I remember the day vividly. It was January 24th 2007 - my birthday - a crisp winter's day. I was doing one of my favourite things, lunching with my father in front of a roaring fire in a quaint Woodstock hotel in Oxfordshire.

This lunch date was different though. Dad did not just pick up the bill; he left having agreed to help fund my grand new scheme. I had persuaded him, in the way that only a loving daughter can, to invest in a run-down pub in a pretty hamlet just outside Worcester.

Six months later, with finances in place and my beautiful barn remortgaged up to the hilt, I opened the doors on a refurbished, shiny dining pub.

Friends and family had worked like Trojans to get the place looking sensational. I was so proud I could have burst.

I had no knowledge of how to run a kitchen, but fate brought me a talented chef. While he created an award winning kitchen, I played hostess. I loved every minute of it.

For the first year, we were blessed with success. I pounded the streets of Worcester and neighbouring villages pushing leaflets through doors.

The marketing worked. The people came to dine and drink wine.

The Office for National Statistics says the 'great recession' hit the country in the second quarter of 2008. It hit a Worcester country pub in the third quarter. In September 2008 out of nowhere. A financial hurricane.

The people stopped coming.

As turnover dropped, it became difficult and at times impossible, to pay staff, utility bills, VAT and suppliers. I remortgaged my house again, borrowed more from my father and emptied my savings.

It was a forlorn battle. Failure to pay suppliers led to a volley of threatening phone calls followed by the charge of the bailiffs.

They attacked like vultures. They invaded the pub, even the house, regardless of time or day. Most of the time courage failed me and I hid, but one clever individual arrived at the pub in the middle of a busy Sunday lunch to ensure he could confront me. I was overcome with shame.

The news kept reminding us that 50 pubs a week were closing.

On the surface I attempted to remain upbeat and positive putting on a brave face for both staff and customers. Mainly I succeeded.

At home, behind closed doors, it was so different. My resolve and resilience were being attacked mercilessly. With a 40 minute drive to the pub and regular 12 hour shifts my body and mind slowly succumbed to exhaustion.

There were times when I could not lift my body from the sofa and the effort of driving the car to the pub became unbearable. Family became worried as I showed signs of being on the edge of a breakdown.

I kept going somehow, for three years, endlessly pumping money into the business. And while there were many tough times there were also moments of sheer joy.

Moments when the team delivered such outstanding food and events (birthdays, anniversaries and weddings) that it made the pain worthwhile.

Moments when the tears in a bride's eyes, when her breath was taken away by the beauty of the building and gardens, brought tears to my own eyes.

Times when I would leave before closing time and look back through the windows to see the candles flickering and see and hear the laughter. I would overflow with pride.

Eventually, my chef moved on to a more 'secure' job. It left me high and dry. I had 22 weddings booked and no chef. It was at that point, while I was at my lowest ebb, that a wolf in human's clothing came in to my life.

With his silky smooth tones and his oh so polite manner he offered his catering services. Specialising in weddings and with testimonials galore he promised that he could provide the catering for the weddings. The happy couples could still have their dream wedding with me and my team still at the helm. A perfect solution.

So confident was I in this man that I allowed him to take over the liaising with the couples about their wedding plans. All seemed to be going well. The relief was huge.

And then disaster. One Saturday evening, two weeks before the first wedding, I received the first of several emails from the wedding couples saying they had been informed that Mr. Wolf was not going to deliver on his promise. He had told them he did not believe the business relationship between the two of us was tenable.

Instinct sent me driving me to the pub the next day like a woman possessed and the instant I arrived I realised something was wrong. As I looked at the garden there was not one piece of garden furniture to be seen. With fear in my heart, I unlocked the front door and froze.

First, the bar. Nothing. Not a single chair or sofa or fridge. All gone.

Then the restaurant. Just an empty cavernous space.

Finally, the kitchen. Just a few wires hanging pathetically from the walls. Stripped to its core. Thousands of pounds of kitchen equipment removed.

Of course I rang the police, but there was nothing they could do. A civil matter apparently. I sought legal advice. Yes I had a good case, but did I want to throw good money after bad? So with a heavy heart I walked away.

Today, the pub is a sorry sight. The garden is overgrown with weeds. Paint is peeling off the woodwork and it looks forlorn. The sound of happy laughter is long gone. Only silence.

Two years on I have finally resurfaced. They have been long difficult years. Years of self-doubt, depression, and a falling out of love with life. Full of times when it felt as though everyone apart from family and friends were against me. I lost everything that was dear to me. The pub, my barn and my marriage.

Last year, when my brother asked me what was keeping me in Warwickshire, I realised I didn't know. When the question was followed by the offer of temporary accommodation, I seized it and moved lock stock and barrel to Somerset.

The move was scary but liberating. I left behind fond memories but also emotionally debilitating ones.

Initially I hid from the world in my brother's attic, but then the day came when I knew I had to venture out.

I started by joining a couple of business networks, which led to my meeting some incredible people. It was empowering.

I went to emotional healing sessions and I started to read voraciously. Anything and everything about healing - of both the body and mind - and the laws of attraction.

Reading 'The Secret' was the big turning point. It made me understand the power of the universe and how it responds to the energy I give out.

Now I work hard at sending out only positive energy. Of course there are times when it is not easy, when I feel the stirrings of self-doubt but in return it has sent special people into my life. Wonderful loving people who are helping and supporting me on the next part of my life's journey and I have let them in.

Like all of us who have told our Bounce Back story my experience has been life changing, but for the better. Now out the other side I shall devote the rest of my working life to helping my clients on their financial journey. I approach it with an insight into people's relationship with money that I did not have before.

Money doesn't buy us happiness, but it does consume us in a bid to achieve our desired lifestyle.

Kassi-Jayne Marshall

Kassi is a self-employed Personal Assistant and Administrator.

After spending years dealing with bullying by students and teachers alike, in her final school year Kassi could only cope with 2 hours a day and was left with low confidence and anxiety issues. However, she left school with 9 GCSEs and a college diploma.

Still lacking confidence, when she started work her anxiety flared and this led to unhappy jobs and yet more pressure.

This is where Kassi took her happiness into her own hands; she sought professional help and started her own business.

Now in charge of her own future, Kassi is less stressed, learning new skills and flourishing!

You can reach Kassi at:

Facebook:
www.facebook.com/TenaciousPA

Twitter:
www.twitter.com/@TenaciousPA

Triumph
By Kassi-Jayne Marshall

Have you ever been the butt of a joke?

How about shouted at?

How about punched in the back?

Had your hair pulled?

Had someone threaten to push you in the school pond?

Strangled?

Slapped?

I'm sure the list could go on, but my hands already shake when I think about it.

For over 14 years of my life, this was what to expect daily.

Before we get into the details, I should start off with saying: I am happy.

My current life is heading down a path that I chose myself, which I worked hard to forge and I am excited to see where it takes me.

I am happy.

So where to start, but the beginning?

In primary school, I had a few close friends and they were my world. I looked forward to going to school each day - I relished in building new relationships and learning new things. We had school assemblies where we'd all sit on the floor, sing songs, listen to the teachers, whisper amongst ourselves and get told off for not listening. I remember talks about how some teachers had received complaints about this thing called "bullying" and that we should all be nice to one another - and that was that.

After a few months when we were all settling in to the routine and enjoying time with our friends, I got called fat. It was by a boy in my class that had barely spoken a word to me since the first day and all of his friends laughed. So I laughed. "She's so fat, she's as fat as the world". He laughed and pointed at my stomach. I laughed along and walked away, confused by the rude thing he said, but everyone laughed so it must be a joke.

I was happy.

After a few years, I knew the word "bully" and the jokes were more frequent. I still had some friends and they laughed too, but still, they were laughing so "it must be a joke". I sat through lessons, ignoring the boy kicking the back of my chair, or the girl whispering to her friend and pointing at me.

I told my mum the "funny" joke the boy told at school and she looked at my dad with unsure eyes. She went to my teachers and that Friday morning we had an assembly about "bullying" and were told to be nice to one another, that was that.

I was happy.

Skip ahead to secondary school. On my first day, mum took a photo by the gate before I went inside to find my new friends. We were given our timetables and sent off to lessons. On the way down the stairs from my first lesson in a swarm of girls hurrying to their next class, I was punched in the back. By the time I turned around, there was nobody behind me. I told my friends and we laughed it off as someone ignorant knocking me with their bag, but you know as well as I do that a bag doesn't feel like a fist. I knew there were people worse off than me, so it couldn't be bullying.

I was confused.

Years on, I knew they weren't joking, I knew who my bullies were and I didn't like school any more. I faked headaches and made my voice hoarse so that mum wouldn't make me go, but she knew I was lying and off I went.

I'd sit in a corner, or bury myself in my small group of friends. I'd pretend it was fine and that I didn't see the face "she" just pulled at me while the rest of them laughed behind her. I'd also pretend that my so-called friends weren't spreading rumours about me and calling me names. I struggled to find an excuse for the time I asked a girl in my class to let me pass her and she replied with a slap to the face.

I was hiding.

By the final year of school, I had been to counselling. I had been to the school nurse so often she didn't believe me anymore and some of the teachers were as bad as the bullies – or worse because they knew better. I'd spend hours in the evenings crying to my parents about what happened. I didn't do my homework because I was busy being physically sick with worry or shying away in my room, crying and begging Mum not to make me go tomorrow.

Some days Mum would drop me at the gate, watch me inside and then as I watched her drive away, I'd hop into the field next door and walk to meet the friends I made outside of school instead.

I was running.

Eventually though, there comes a day where everybody snaps. My mum snapped when a girl held me over the school pond, threatening to let go and drop me in. Before I knew it, I had run through the gates, down the road and a mile away to cry at my Nans' front door.

Mum and I had a meeting with my doctor and the school liaison: my anxiety was affecting my work and health so I would be allowed to school for 2 hours a day. We worked my schedule to fit in the most important lessons and I took the rest of my work home. I had few friends left, but that didn't matter because I would be leaving soon - I wasn't going to sixth form anyway.

One day, I was in my tutor room trying to print off some work and the girls kept turning my computer off. Enough was enough; it was my turn to snap. I threw the computer keyboard at the wall, swore at them to go away and ran out of the room, shaking and crying with anger. I stumbled down the stairs to find the teacher and ask him to let me go home. I explained about the girls and nothing was done.

I was terrified.

Finally, the day came where I'd sat my last exam and the results showed that I had done well enough to go to college to study for a BTEC.

I was ecstatic at the chance to leave behind the horrible jokes, sneers, slaps and punches from my school life. After all, students at college are more grown up than those at school, right?

Wrong.

Queue another 2 years of names, jokes, tears and running away. On two occasions I sat down with my course tutors and told them I was leaving. By now, I had learned that jokes aren't always funny and "friends" aren't always friends.

I was depressed.

After college came work, more stress, more know-it-all bosses, more misunderstanding and more anxiety. One boss accused me of gross misconduct due to a discrepancy in my timesheet thanks to an incorrect clock in a hallway - something one of the staff later admitted to. Another said my gastric flu was 'nothing but a hangover' and fired me on the spot (I sarcastically wondered if they would have preferred me vomiting in the restaurant). I didn't even bother giving them the doctor's note I had excluding me from work.

I was exhausted.

One evening after work, I was sat at home talking to Mum, crying (this is starting to sound familiar, isn't it?) about the panic attack I had at work that day, wondering if it was ever going to get better.

I had seen jobs work for other people, so why was it so hard for me?

It was then that Mum suggested I go self-employed. I had done some short-term administrative work in the past and really thrived in that environment. I had watched her set up her own business while my sister and I were at school, so why couldn't I do it too?

The more I thought about it, the more it made sense. I started doing some odd jobs for friends and family and it was like I had found my calling. In early 2014, I picked a name and took the plunge. Tenacious PA was official.

We come to today. I sit here, the proud owner of my own business, working hours that fit the life I am building. I work a few days a week in my Granddad's office and divide the rest between amazing clients, friends and myself. I still struggle with depression and anxiety, but thanks to my family and my real friends I can cope.

I could get upset about the horrible people I dealt with when I was younger. I could point fingers and throw blame until I'm blue in the face, but I am slowly letting go of them. I may never forgive them truly; I don't think I want to. Instead, I choose to thrive. I am learning to love myself for all the things they refused to see.

I choose to pass on my experience with my head held high and hope that others can learn from my story.

I want you to learn to laugh at jokes that are funny, not at your expense.

I want you to learn that just because someone 'has it worse' doesn't mean you can't be upset.

I want you to learn that you are human, real and deserving and no one should have the power to make you feel like you're not.

I want you to learn to love yourself.

I have learned that I deserve better.

I am valid.

I choose to be **happy**.

Laura Barnett

Laura is all about Freedom To Live! Running her own businesses since 2007, after 10 unpredictable years in marketing, she sought to do something that would provide her with the freedom and independence she craved and most importantly everyday happiness.

At the heart of Laura's diverse skills is the desire to help people succeed in enjoying life and achieving their goals. Through business development, health and wellbeing education, lifestyle coaching and teaching martial arts, she strives to help others design a life to their ideals.

You can reach Laura at:

Email:
choices@freedomtolive.co.uk

Website:
www.freedomtolive.co.uk

Twitter:
www.twitter.com/freedom_to_live

Life Is Like A Yo-Yo
By Laura Barnett

"Where's my suitcase?"

Three words that will forever remind me of June 2015. Headed to Marbella for a family celebration, eight of us have just piled out of the taxi at Gatwick. It's 7am. This is where it begins. Instant panic ensues – we check all the luggage on the pavement with Mel, ticking off individual cases, buggies, car seats, and pushchairs! "No, it's not here – the big black suitcase with all the children's clothes, sunscreen, toiletries, and my wardrobe. It's still on the landing."

Quick as a flash her husband Paul makes a decision to call the taxi back, return home, pick it up and meet us all in departures. Into task mode straight away Mel dials the taxi, Paul ferrets in the nappy change bag for his passport and boarding pass and we all agree to get checked-in and ready for the flight, which takes off in just over two and half hours! No problem – the house is only sixty minutes away via the M25! In less than ten minutes taxi man is back and Paul's jumped in and gone, with a wave and parting comment of "See you at the gate, it'll be fine". The rest of us – two couples and Mel, with her two children under four, are gathering various paraphernalia off the pavement and delegating responsibilities including managing a toddler on a Trunki and a crying baby in a pushchair! I don't have a watch, but I know time is of the essence.

Through the airport double doors, chaos and noise hit the senses. We scan the TV screens displaying hundreds of options for flights to destinations all over the world. The trusted orange flashes of Squeezyjet shows itself as zone C, with long waiting lines announcing the designated area for cheap and cheerful, holidaymakers like us. We join the queue and slowly meander our way around the snaking barriers. Time is ticking along, every five minutes there's an urgent shout from a uniformed member of staff clutching a list of flights departing shortly. Debates bubble in the queue assessing the various inefficiencies of the process and the laborious task of simply getting your luggage on-board.

An hour's now slipped by, another two desks open, causing a stir of excitement among the waiting travellers. "It'll be fine," was heard echoing through the hustle and bustle. We reach the front, staying together, checking the cases. Turns out two of us didn't even need to hang about with hand luggage but hey, we're all together and the word from Paul is he's got the suitcase and he's back on the motorway! We tell the uniformed lady of his late arrival – lost passport being the more legitimate excuse put forward. She instructs us to send him to the front desk as soon as he arrives. Great, it'll be fine!

Next stop, security. We get to the designated family access point, allegedly designed to be quicker, but the pace we're going certainly doesn't feel like it. The queue moves painfully slowly, time is ticking along and we finally reach the conveyor. Things are bundled into boxes ready for scanning – shoes, belts, phones, socks, wallets, carry-ons, cosmetics – all laid out on display. I'm first through, no beeps. Next, John my other half; then the parents; and finally the pushchair with Mel, baby Oliver and four year old Oscar. All clear. Phew. But a second look shows most of our bags have been separated for a further security check. Turns out the iPad should have been removed too. Mum and Dad are unaware of the 100ml liquid rule. Still packed in their hand luggage and also over the maximum limit, mum watches despondently as sun cream, after perfume, after moisturiser gets unceremoniously thrown in the bin. For her, that's about fifty of her hard earned pounds just disregarded. With murmured sounds of agitation, about 1kg lighter and another fifteen minutes later, we're fully clothed and only waiting for the baby food to be checked. All clear, Mel is now sorted, belongings gathered and children strapped in. She's quite calm considering.

Onto the departure lounge. We're looking forward to coffee, breakfast, a pee and perhaps some shopping. Mel's phone chimes with a message, Paul's nearing the M23 junction no more than a few miles away – he's going to make it.

All the while, Oliver's been whiney, but he'll have to wait a bit longer. There's been nothing dramatic with either little one, no tantrums or disasters just a few odd smells, hungry grizzles and typical toddler attention needs. "What's the time?" I ask as we head into the main hubbub. I've already seen the departure board flashing 'last call' on our flight. With the knowledge that our appointed gate is a fair step away and that Mel needs to get nappies changed and bottles of water replaced, I thought a gentle question would be prudent to focus our next steps. Time's running out.

We stride through the frenzy of duty free shopping toward the gates. Luckily, we're not the furthest away. Once there, we notify more orange clad staff that Paul will be here. His name is taken as our passports and boarding passes get checked again and the bus pulls up outside to take us off to the Tarmac. We let everyone else pile on first, we've got excess baggage: pushchairs to collapse, car seats to carry and bags to be re-organised. Since those three little words were uttered just two and a half hours ago, we've not stopped! Mel's phone is just about audible over Oliver and Oscar's constant chattering and the hundreds of people filing past us to the bus. It's Paul.

He's been refused check-in at the front desk.

Too late.

Gate is closing.

If only he hadn't had that suitcase to check-in!

Remarkably, Mel is still calm.

What do we do now? Everything's not fine.

The only option is to go ahead without him. We're the last to board the bus. It takes us ten minutes to reach the aircraft, another ten to board and then another forty, before we actually depart due to a maintenance issue! He could probably have made it in all honesty, but here we are now cruising at 37,000 feet – a man down and not knowing when we'll be reunited! We can't worry from up here, so let's enjoy the fact we can sit down and finally have that coffee and breakfast. I'm wondering what on earth Mel must be feeling at this point. After forgetting the bag, now missing her husband and dealing with the kids single-handedly, I put my head back to contemplate and listen to some tunes. Suddenly, there's a commotion next to me – it's Oliver, he's been sick... all over Mel! She laughs and grabs the wet-wipes.

So what's the point of my story, which forms only the first few hours of a weeklong family holiday? It's that stuff happens. Whether we like it or not, things go wrong. This is an extreme example, I appreciate that. How many challenges do we actually face in any single day? Forgetting the school lunchbox, taking a wrong turn, choosing what to have for dinner, finding the right outfit, juggling deadlines, losing keys, feeling poorly or an unexpected bill. Have you ever sat and really thought about it? If you did, how many of those challenges would you actually just take in your stride, find a solution and move on?

Each and every day we are faced with numerous challenges, some greater and more difficult, exciting or terrifying than others. Each with their own unique and individual impact on day-to-day living. Some short, some long. Some major, some minor. It would be wholly unrealistic of me to suggest that life is perfect – a lot of it is out of our control. But what I can say, categorically, is that where there is Ying, there is Yang. Whatever bad stuff happens there also has to be good.

Just like a yo-yo, when you're in control of it, it rolls down the string and naturally springs back up. And the same is true of life. You're in control of the ups and the downs. You have the power to manage exactly how impactful they are. If you choose not to be in control and to let the yo-yo hang aimlessly on its string, you will struggle to find the momentum to spring it back up.

That's what bounce means to me. It's the knowledge, not only that there is always a positive to a negative, but also that we have innate 'BOUNCEBACKABILITY'. We can deal with anything. It's just that very often we don't even recognise the challenges that we've faced and overcome – let alone give ourselves a pat on the back for it.

Why not take a moment? Look at your day today, or yesterday and really think about the challenges you were presented with, small or large, and how you overcame them. Give yourself some credit where it's due and see that you are in control of your yo-yo. You have the power within you to spring back up whenever you choose to.

And, in case you're wondering...

Paul arrived 4 hours later on another flight. We didn't get the right hire car, got lost on the toll road to the villa and it turned out that Oliver had a tummy bug. Yet, despite all that, we did have a lovely family holiday together and Mel never let anything get her down!

Laurie Vallas

Laurie has been a writer all her life – beginning, as many do – with a diary. Inspired by an English teacher in High School, she began to observe life more closely and subsequently developed both a habit and a hobby of making copious notes about ordinary circumstances.

One observation in particular is Laurie's ability to see heart shapes – everywhere. Sometimes in fallen leaves, oftentimes in clouds, occasionally in cinnamon-swirl toast and frequently discovered amidst the stones at her feet. Finding the heart in everything was the inspiration behind "The Heartifacts": the business of getting to the core of all that matters. The Heartifacts facilitates the discovery of valuable, hidden potential within organizations, communities and individuals.

For years, Laurie's family has encouraged her to write 'her book' – and this is a start. Laurie currently lives in the US with her husband Larry and their cats Wilson and Fiona, but considers her home – naturally, where her heart is.

You can reach Laurie at:

Website:
www.theheartifacts.com

LinkedIn:
Laurie Vallas

Facebook:
The Heartifacts and PositiviTEAs

Twitter:
@TheHeartifacts

Great Expectations
By Laurie Vallas

I expected to be a mother one day. Not hoped, not planned – expected. In fact, in my late 20's, I was so confident about this I had offered to donate eggs to a friend who was struggling to conceive. You can imagine when, in my late 30's and nothing had 'happened' yet, I started to become... concerned. In the meantime, I continued to focus on developing my career.

I was stunned the day I landed my dream job, I couldn't believe it! It was in organizational improvement and I was elated beyond expression. A few days later, I paused long enough to realize I was 'late'. When the little blue '+' appeared I felt I had finally landed my 'other' dream job!

I could hardly contain my excitement. I wanted to tell the world and yet the first few days of joy and disbelief were interrupted with moments of concern about 'how could I have both?'

Thinking back, I shudder at how ridiculous I was to even consider these to be parallel achievements.

Then, the day came when the decision was made for me. Four days before Christmas. I felt as though my Soul was pouring out of me and there was nothing I could do to stop it. Nothing.

That was a dark time.

It was dark until I started talking to other women. I was shocked by how common miscarriages are. I am not suggesting that a few conversations fixed everything, but it was certainly a start in my bouncing back.

Months later, my husband and I met with the top fertility doctor in the area. After some tests, it was determined that given my age and uncertain egg quality, I had about a 20-30% IVF success rate. Again, I was disappointed, but undaunted. I began researching for evidence that this was not entirely impossible.

Things were on an upward swing and one random summer Saturday morning my husband asked me, "What if we adopted? What if we adopted a little boy and his sister?" I thought my heart would burst right out of my chest! I never thought he would have been open to that sort of thing. I immediately ran for the computer and registered for the next information session and started to study all I needed to know about the adoption process.

Months passed before I heard anything. Finally I arrived home to a letter from one of the adoption agencies inviting us to an information session. Unfortunately, the date fell when we would be away. I panicked. Immediately, I phoned to see if there would be other sessions – to understand if this would be the only session we were eligible for, etc. This was new to me and I was willing to drop everything to avoid disqualification from this critical step.

The social worker proceeded to ask a series of questions, which I thought was odd, given I was mainly inquiring about future information sessions. However, assuming this was normal protocol, I answered everything. The questions were probing, personal and provocative. When asked if I'd ever miscarried, the pain seized me like it was happening all over again. She pressed on. The momentum was such that there seemed to be no opportunity to halt this slow-moving train-wreck, fast approaching my now-battered heart. I could hardly speak.

Finally, the questioning stopped and she concluded with, "I think it would be best if you contacted an organization called 'More to Life,' as I don't think you or your husband are qualified to adopt..."

I don't remember much after that. It was a Friday, and my husband arrived home to an empty, dehydrated, crushed shell of a being. I was wailing, hard. The noises emitting from me were completely foreign. The miscarriage seemed easier.

I did not move from my bed for five days. The social worker's words pierced my head like nails sealing a coffin. All I could think about was that there may be no more point to my life.

Initially, talking about the experience was excruciating to relive. It took six months to put myself back to some sort of togetherness; a lot of help came from a myriad of therapists, healers and dear girlfriends.

Then, a letter arrived. It was another invitation to an information session.

I began to tremble.

Suddenly I found myself dialling their number.

"Hello, this is X – how can I help?"

"I received an invitation to an information session. I would like to meet with the head of your organization. When are they available?"

"Of course. When would you be available?"

"Right now."

(Startled) "Please hold a moment... The Director would be free at 11am tomorrow. Would that suit?"

"Thank you. Yes, I will be there."

I hung up.

I am not known for my punctuality; however I was sitting in the carpark at 10.25am, running scenarios through my mind. What did I want to say? How could I approach this so that the outcome would be of the most value? How could I take this outrageous situation and turn it into something positive for myself, the organization, the children, other prospective and hopeful parents?

The Director had the kindest face and the loveliest of dispositions. She reminded me of both Olivia Newton John and Lindsay Wagner; women I imagined to be approachable and gentle. Lucky for her.

This gave me a stable platform from which to construct a rational conversation. I began by asking her to describe normal protocol for someone phoning to inquire about dates of upcoming information sessions. She asked me to enlighten her of my experience – so I asked:

- Is a full, spontaneous personality assessment of the prospective adoptive mother part of that inquiry about dates?

- Is a sight-unseen, speculative assessment and value-judgement about the prospective adoptive father – typical?

- Is it usual for the social worker to persist with difficult and deeply sensitive questioning to the point where the caller is in distress – and can no longer speak?

- Is it normal protocol to then add, "You probably need to accept that this process is not for you" – only to rush them off the phone to, presumably, wrap up their day, and go home to their family?

- Is it not part of your due-diligence and respect for the human being on the other end of the line – when a conversation has escalated to that level of angst – to not provide a follow-up call to see if they are ok?

By this time, I was sitting squarely in front of her. Unexpectedly, she appeared to take on my persona – physically curled up as if she were right there on the other end of the phone. She looked helpless; just as I was six months earlier.

She asked if I wanted the social worker to join the meeting. At first, I said no, but then, I felt it was my responsibility to stay the course, follow through with my intended resolution – and leave things better than I found them.

The social worker joined, and before she could say anything, I asked, "Have you ever experienced a miscarriage?" "Yes", she replied.

"How did that feel? Do you remember? Do you remember when that happened? Do you…"

"It was a long time ago," she replied abruptly.

"How many women do you speak to in a typical week? Do you even remember speaking to me? Did you ever consider the impact your conversation had on my life? Would it matter to you that I lost five days of my life because of your insensitive and inaccurate assessment of our ability to be good parents? Did you even think about me after you hung up – or was that just another day's work? I wanted to take my own life after that call. Did it ever occur to you how many other women's dreams have been crushed by your callousness? Has anyone ever come back for a discussion like this after a phone call like the one I had with you? Do you ever check the statistics of suicides that may have been related to calls to people like you? By the way, do you have a daughter?"

"Yes – and no, no one has come back…"

"How would you feel if your daughter was treated the way you have treated me?"

Silence.

The Director sat motionless in her chair, weeping quietly.

"I am here because I shudder to think of how many people may have been mistreated by this process. I am here because not everyone has the tools and resources I did to put my shattered heart and broken dreams back together; to pull myself together and come back to look you both in the eye and demand that you not treat couples like this ever again. I am here to put both a face and a voice to all the other women and men who, like me, were totally crushed by your insensitive practice and who did not have it in them to come back to you and demand change. Are you aware of how much effort goes into arriving at a decision like this? To stop trying to make a baby – and to instead, make a life – a family, for parentless children?"

After a long pause and a few sombre conclusions, the shaken social worker excused herself for a meeting. I had clearly made my point.

As the Director walked me to the door, she timidly asked, "Would it be ok to contact you in six months or so, to…?" I stopped her mid-sentence and replied, "No thank you. Please remove us from your mailing list and apologize to the children in your care because unfortunately they will never have the benefit of having been raised by two exceptionally loving people. However I am hopeful that future couples coming to you will now be treated with the individual dignity and respect they deserve and the children in your care will be placed into their loving homes, very soon."

Perhaps I could have been gentler – but that day, the women and men who were turned away before me, were now vindicated. The meeting drew a line in the sand for those that came after me. I have since realized that this very action was what any mother would have done in defence of her children. I did not have to give birth to awaken my natural maternal instincts. Taking that stand and challenging the status quo was the best gift I could give to those children. I was born to make a difference, and if my purpose is to plant seeds of change that bloom and bear future fruits; then I am a mother after all.

At the time, I never believed I could pull through – never thought I could talk about this experience constructively. I did. I can. I am now able to offer a soft landing for others. Together, we can help each other bounce back!

Leni Miller

Leni is one of life's survivors. She left home too young, which led to a spiraling life of drugs, bad abusive relationships and eating disorders. She jumped from job to job leaving her confidence in tatters.

Major surgery left Leni with chronic pain and life on a daily cocktail of debilitating painkillers.

Leni now lives in Wiltshire with her soul mate and husband of 14 years, Mike, and Mr. Bo Bo Baggins, her beloved English Bulldog. She is trained in NLP and uses the Law of Attraction to manifest health, wealth, and the successful career she now enjoys.

Leni is passionate about helping others use these simple techniques to manifest the same.

You can reach Leni at:

Email:
lenimanifestmiller@gmail.com

Facebook:

https://facebook.com/leni.haylett

The Transformation Of A Troubled Mind
By Leni Miller

Leaving home at an early age really seemed like a good idea at the time. This wasn't really a choice though. I grew up Daddy's little girl, where I worshipped my father and we did everything together. When my parents ended their relationship, it left me at home alone with my mother. We always had an incredibly strained relationship where no matter what I did it was nowhere near good enough. The barrage of negativity and constant humiliation was too much for me. I filled a rucksack full of clothes and left.

I was homeless. This was not something I had ever anticipated at such a young age and clearly I was not prepared. For a while I slept on friends' floors with an immense sense of insecurity, not knowing where to go or what to do. I finally found a pokey bed-sit. It was small, dimly lit and smelt musty, but it had a bed.

I found it difficult to keep a job. I was a child, I had no sense of respect and I was full of pure unadulterated anger against anyone who would challenge me. This was how I protected myself without realising the detrimental effect it had on my life.

I found solace in drugs. These would incapacitate me to the point where I was always late for work; hence the lack of gainful employment. The drugs were numbing and for those brief moments of being high, I felt that life couldn't be better. Time was physically non-existent while on drugs; I didn't have to face my challenges, as I felt euphoric in every sense. It was my way to be "non-physical" in the world I had created, which was filled with self-pity, self-loathing and total worthlessness.

Drugs were my sanctuary from the enormous, encapsulating feeling of being totally alone. One of my lowest times involved me having just enough money on Christmas Day to get a pack of 10 cigarettes and a sausage roll. I sat in my bed and cried all day, watching ants on my floor milling around without a care in the world. I was so exhausted from crying, I couldn't muster up the energy to get rid of them.

Things had to get better, there had to be more to life! I finally managed to reduce the drugs, but I needed something to replace them. I needed to control something and I had unfortunately always been a very picky eater. This developed into various eating disorders, starting with anorexia. Looking back, being a size 6/8 at a height of 5"9 wasn't attractive. At the time, I didn't care though, I felt fat and I did something about it.

I trained twice a day and I trained hard. I ate as little as I could get away with and surprisingly this was easy to hide from others. I even went to see a hypnotist to see if I could be hypnotised into eating healthy foods; alas it didn't work for me. She gave me a video of "The Secret", I watched about 20 minutes and didn't think much of it.

This rapid destruction of confidence also led to abusive relationships. After an ex-partner was arrested for assaulting me, I spent an exhausting 6 hours going through statements with the police until 5am. I couldn't sleep, but I couldn't stop my mind wandering either.

Whilst lying in bed reviewing my doomed future, I felt the urge to go to Waterstones bookstore. I was up, ready and waiting for the doors to open that morning. I wandered aimlessly through the spiritual and self-help sections desperate for answers. I came away with a few books on Witchcraft and something called "The Law of Attraction".

I liked the idea of just "think and imagine things are better". However, I struggled with the actual practise of this. I still read the books and they came in very handy when playing charades with friends. I was a winner every time! I do have very fond memories of watching friends attempting "What to Say When You Talk to Yourself," "To Ride a Silver Broomstick", or "New Generation Witchcraft". Trust me, it's beyond hilarious.

My next adventure was my health. One sunny Thursday morning I was in pain, nothing too serious. However, I thought I would go to the doctor to get checked out. Within 4 hours, I was at the hospital having pelvic surgery to remove a cyst 9cm in diameter from my ovaries. Your ovaries are only the size of a walnut, so having a foreign body triple in size clinging on and draining all life is not a good feeling.

Being fit and healthy, I recovered quite quickly. That being said, I was left with another little surprise: incredibly painful pelvic adhesions. Adhesions are scar tissue, which sticks your organs together causing an ocean of horrendous abdominal pain. So far, I have had close to 9 surgeries for division of the adhesions and endless ruptured cysts. More surgery means more adhesions, which equate to living a life of constant chronic pain.

Over 10 years I suffered, living life on Cocodamol, Tramadol, Pethadine and Oramorph. The unfortunate downside is that you build up a tolerance, so you need stronger painkillers. When that doesn't work, you double dose as the pain is excruciating and debilitating. I missed out on so much life due to being incapacitated from either the pain or the drugs.

You sit and slowly watch the colour drain from the world around you. Not knowing what kind of day you could have is depressing. Will I be able to make it downstairs today? Will I be able to shower? Can I make it to work? Another unfortunate side effect of some of the drugs was weight gain, 4 stone of it. For someone with eating disorders, this could not get any worse. You can't exercise due to the pain and you can't exercise on morphine, as coordination is a basic requirement in kickboxing.

It was time for me to watch "The Secret" again, and this time actually watch it all the way through! It really isn't madness; if you do the same thing, you get the same results. I needed to do something different otherwise my life would be doomed.

I started to change my awareness, of myself and of my entire surroundings. This was a slow process and it really took a great deal of practise to start with. To my surprise, day by day, slowly things did start to change. I believe life is what you make it.

I found a career in sales and client management. Maybe things were working! I realised I was exceptional at it and it gave me the capacity to help people. This unfortunately came with yet another demon - other sales people. You see when you do well in life, it tends to highlight others' limitations. I was incredibly successful in all my job roles, but I was not liked. I used to think it was just me, that my personality didn't fit in. I struggled through the jealousy and back stabbing to the point where I quadrupled my income in the space of one year. I finally found techniques that worked for me and visualised finding people I could help.

I wanted a house of my own, however it was during the 2009 credit crunch. I had no deposit, even so, my partner and I went house hunting anyway. We found a property that was perfect and we made an offer. Unfortunately we were too late and an offer had been accepted from another couple. Now, at this point we didn't even have a mortgage agreed, however that's not the way that manifesting works.

I continued to pack up my current house into boxes. My partner thought I was completely barking mad, and would go around unpacking after me! I asked the estate agent to contact me first once the other couple pulled out and he promptly laughed in my face. Every evening I would visualise walking over the threshold of my new house carrying boxes.

I wrote my name and the address of the new house on envelopes repeatedly every day. Two weeks later, I went shopping to DFS to find a new sofa to go in the conservatory of the new house and I received a call from the estate agent "tentatively" asking if I was still interested.

A few days later, the buyer pulled out and disappeared off the face of the earth. We made an offer, which was accepted. I still hadn't even thought about the deposit and only got that sorted 5 days before it was due to be paid! You just concentrate on the end goal.

I am now blissfully married to my soul mate who is my "port in a storm". I realised that sometimes you have to go through the bad ones to contrast when you find that good person and then you can be grateful for them. I realised everything is possible if you believe it. If you don't believe it, then start to pretend instead.

Visualise your outcome every day for 5 minutes. Your brain does not know the difference between reality and fiction. It only knows your dominant thoughts. I learned that the emotion of happiness feels so much better than sadness or anger.

Through my transformation, I am complete just the way I am. Being more aware of how I talk to myself helped me lose that 4 stone, it helped me eat better, and it helped me manage my pain.

I met others with similar mindsets, who have become dear friends and I am now no longer alone.

Letisha Galloway

Letisha Galloway is an international bestselling author, book coach, poet, and speaker. She is the co-author of When New Life Begins, Family Ties: What Binds Us and Tears Us Apart, The Missing Piece: A Life Transformed, and The Missing Piece in Forgiveness. Letisha authored a book titled Victim to Victor: A Story of Love, Failure and Faith which chronicles her life as an abandoned child, domestic violence survivor, losing her only child, and many other life changing events.

Letisha is regularly involved in bringing awareness to domestic violence. Letisha is active in child abuse prevention activities. Additionally Letisha advocates for the homeless and ending hunger.

You can reach Letisha at:

Email:
letisha.nicole@gmail.com

Website:
www.letisha.galloway.com

Facebook:

https://www.facebook.com/letisha.galloway

https://www.facebook.com/authorletishagalloway

Twitter:

https://twitter.com/letisha_nicole

Believing In Me
By Letisha Galloway

I arrived into this world with a major challenge. I was born with deformed legs that were amputated when I was less than a year old. I was raised by my maternal great-grandmother. At a very early age I was labelled as learning disabled. As a double amputee, I felt insecure. I questioned if I was a complete person at times. I had things in my heart that I wanted to do, but simply was not physically able to. I was my own worst critic.

When the children would run track, I would have to walk and that was frustrating to me. Visually I could see myself running, yet when it came down to it physically it just wasn't happening. I would spend hours in my backyard practicing running. After a while I got up to a jog, but it still wasn't the run that I desired. The inferiority that I felt was deeply rooted, so much so that people didn't even know it existed. I was an expert at hiding my insecurity behind my smiles, jokes, and laughter. My insecurity got worse in the third grade.

I was labeled learning disabled in the second grade. I was moved from a private school to a public school where I could receive help. The help I received wasn't enough because I repeated the third grade. Entering into special education classes further fuelled my feelings of inferiority. I knew that I didn't belong in all special education classes but I was too afraid to speak up. Although I did belong in the classes for math I didn't have a problem with my other subjects. My issue was that I was bored and distracted.

Along the way I decided that I would just accept the label I had been given.

One teacher in middle school noticed that I completed my work quickly and then would disrupt the class by talking to my friends. She told me that she didn't think I belonged in her class. She gave me a pep talk before telling me that I could test out of her class. She had me retested and I passed all subjects except for math. I was happy to be going to classes with the rest of my classmates. My happiness was short lived because in high school I received more labels.

When I entered high school I was preoccupied with 'girl talk' and roaming the halls with my friends while looking for cute boys. My ninth grade report card wasn't stellar. I had mostly B's, C's, and a few D's. Most of the teenagers began to see the guidance counselors about college preparation. I made an appointment to see the guidance counselor as well and was told that I was not college material and that I should consider trade school. I understood that my grades were not good enough.

At the end of ninth grade I discovered that my great-grandmother was diagnosed with cancer. I was devastated. One day she told me that she knew that I could have better grades and that she always sees other parents with, "My child is an honor roll student" bumper sticker for their vehicles. I decided right then that I would stop playing around and get her that bumper sticker.

In the tenth grade I became serious about my education. I had entered trade school for part of the day as my guidance counselor suggested. I was in a pre-nursing program. The program was designed to give the foundation needed for a career in nursing. At the end of the school year I had the highest grade in the school and took part in an honorary banquet. At my high school I made the honor roll for all four marking periods. My great-grandmother received her bumper stickers. I placed one on her car. The others I had to place on a door because she was no longer able to drive.

She died later that year. I was devastated. I didn't know how I would make it without her. I remembered that she told me that I could do great things. I held on to what she said and went back to my guidance counselor to talk about college. Again I was told that I was not college material. I was disappointed. A few weeks later, I decided that I would ask for another guidance counselor. I wasn't sure my request would be granted, but to my surprise and excitement it was.

My new guidance counselor was more positive than the last. She told me that if I really applied myself I could make it into college. I believed her and I was excited. My excitement turned into disappointment when I took the college placement test and needed pre-college math and reading comprehension classes before taking on college courses.

Upon entering my first class at the community college I felt embarrassed. In high school I received decent grades, but I was in a non-college level class. I knew exactly why I didn't pass the reading comprehension portion of the placement test. I had taken medication prior to the exam for my allergies and I was not focused. Additionally, the reading material was not interesting. I didn't care about rocks or anything science related.

After I completed the pre-college classes I felt good. I started my college life with expectations of great things to come. I received the dean's list my first few semesters. I excelled and then it all came to a standstill when my long masked depression made an appearance. The pain of past experiences in my life began to take over my daily thought process. I started to think that I couldn't be anything in life. I told myself that the labels people gave me were correct and that I would always be a failure. I started to miss classes. While I was attending classes, people told me that I wouldn't finish. I internalized all of my self-doubt and their opinions and started to self-destruct.

My situation went from bad to worse and even more horrid than that. My vehicle stopped working. I was unable to get to my classes. I had to withdraw. I ended up getting another vehicle and started to come out of my depression, or so I thought. I made the dean's list another semester. However the following semester I was placed on academic probation. The dean of students asked me what was bothering me and I was unable to articulate the pain I felt inside. Eventually I lost my financial aid.

After I lost my financial aid I started to give up. Some days I would stay in my bed all day and cry. I would get tired from crying and fall asleep and then wake up and cry again. My depression was getting out of control and I knew I needed help. Treatment was not new to me. I had seen counselors since I was a child due to parental abandonment issues and the deep sadness I felt because of it. I knew that there was nothing to be afraid of so I decided to go seek help.

One day I made a complete change and moved to another state. On my way to a relative's house, I saw a local community college. I stopped in and got an application and I went into the financial aid office. I explained to the worker that I had experienced some setbacks, but was ready to get my life in order. I told her about my loss of financial aid and she told me that it wouldn't be a problem since I was in a new state at a new college. I was elated.

At the new community college, I flourished. I graduated two years after I started and graduated cum laude. I transferred to a four year university where I finished a bachelor's degree in Criminal Justice. A year after I graduated from the university, I went back to complete a master's degree in Administration of

Human Services with honors. I am currently completing my second masters in Administration of Justice with a 3.77 out of 4.0 grade point average. I look at my accomplishments and wonder how I ever doubted myself.

One of the missing pieces to my bouncing back was embracing who I am. I eventually embraced that I was a beautiful human being just the way God intended me to be. When we embrace who we were created to be, we find freedom. We find the freedom to be unique, to create new paths, and to follow our destiny.

Another missing piece to my bouncing back was believing in my own ability. I spent a lot of time caring about the opinion of others. I wasted a lot of time and energy worrying about how to prove other people wrong. Instead, I should have focused on proving things to myself. I no longer worry myself with the opinions of others. There will always be people who speak negatively about anything positive that you want to do. Some people will never be happy for you, and that is ok.

It is important to realize that you have many gifts and talents that were given to you. It is acceptable to not be like everyone else and to go against the grain.

Everyone has different abilities. Today I am free. Find your missing piece and you will find your freedom.

Liz Walton

NO ... it's impossible ... at 46 ... why now? ... after so long ... 10 year fertility journey ... letting go completely!

Liz is English, but grew up overseas in Africa, South America and the Middle East until she was 14 and moved back to Bath.

She married in 2005 and mistakenly assumed that children would follow.

Her passion for self-healing and exploring potentiality drove her to seek further and deeper.

As therapist, Coach and leader specialising in Fertility, Grief, Depression & Abuse, she knows all deep pain can heal.

This has been her journey!

You can reach Liz at:

Website:
www.lizwalton.org

Facebook:
https://www.facebook.com/LizWaltonTherapiesandCoaching

LinkedIn:
Elizabeth Walton

Twitter:
@lizwalton_heals

Email:
liz@lizwalton.org

Making The Impossible Possible!
By Liz Walton

This is my story. It is a story about the painful journey of infertility and the steps I took to heal myself and learn to live again.

I was never really child oriented, but always assumed that when the time was right I would get married and have kids. It took moving to Africa, where I had the time of my life to meet a man of substance, an Australian, Greg, who I married in England in 2005. I was 35 years old! We moved to Australia settling in Canberra with great jobs and the intention of investing in property and starting a family. Another year went by with nothing happening, so off to the doctor I went. Now aged 37 I was immediately referred to the fertility clinic. There the tests started, lots of tests, invasive and uncomfortable tests, tests I never knew existed, and along with those tests the constant reference to my age. I did not expect that, I still felt 20!

Although I had never been a child orientated person before, the more I found out I couldn't have children the more I wanted them. I was looking at the world through a child centric magnifying glass with everyone being pregnant, having children, or talking about children. There were babies everywhere! My heightened painful sense of being began questioning. Why does everyone make it look so easy? Why do they have them and I don't? What's wrong with me? It was so painful and I felt useless and questioned my identity. Who am I if I can't have children? What is my purpose? Slowly madness crept in and this tunnel vision of children was all I could see. I became obsessed with my fertility and felt Greg was not trying hard enough. I was angry and blamed him.

Referrals, tests, and results take time and months passed. I learned about health, temperature, nutrition, ovulation, hormones, and monthly cycles. I learned about what to do and what not to do. I did my best to do it all believing the key must be here somewhere. There was nothing medically wrong with me, just my age. So it was time to test Greg, a simple, very quick non evasive sperm test! Oh the simplicity of the male reproductive system! The result was anti sperm antibodies. Lots of them all clumping together and not going anywhere near my eggs!

Our option was IVF, an ICSI cycle which involved hormone drugs, lots of injections, numerous tests, and checks for hormone levels. When my eggs were deemed suitably plump and fertile they were harvested and the mature eggs identified. After a cleaning process the best sperm were selected and injected into the egg. Five days later providing the cells had divided correctly the fertilized egg was put back into my body and the two week wait began, the longest two weeks of our lives. Then the inevitable crushing blow was delivered. "No, I am so sorry it didn't work this time." I didn't hear those soul destroying words once, or twice, but rather six times over an eight year period. With each IVF cycle I became increasingly hormonal, increasingly emotional and increasingly desperate. After each failure I gained 2 kilos as I felt so empty and turned to food. I also spent money, money on courses and books. I needed to learn more, to know more and to be more! It is impossible to accurately convey how demoralising this was or the detrimental effect it had on our marriage. We loved each other but were growing apart, I wanted more from Greg but although he could appreciate my pain his mechanism for coping with his own devastation was to throw himself into building his business.

Despite being told that Greg's sperm was the problem, each failed cycle caused me to question what issues I needed to look at. Those issues weren't visible, measurable or external. They were all internal and required healing. Over those eight years I did everything I possibly could to look inside myself and heal myself on a cellular level. There was nothing I wasn't prepared to face, learn or overcome to find the key. There was sexual abuse I never dealt with, depression I ran away from, self-loathing I had masked through self-medicating with lots of drugs, and grief I had not processed. It was time to heal myself. How could I, as a therapist, help people to heal themselves if I couldn't heal myself?

I found The Journey by Brandon Bays which changed my life immeasurably to the point that I did the full practitioners certificate. I loved this work and used it on myself often. In order to heal myself I read every self-help book I could find. I also learnt hypnotherapy to trainer level, NLP up to Trainer Training level and took courses on numerous subjects including energy healing, Australian flower essences, Gestalt therapy, TLT and emotional healing. Greg came on some courses which challenged him terribly. One particular emotional healing course completely changed our relationship and for that I am truly thankful. As I healed I became a stronger, healthier, happier, and more confident, albeit still childless, person.

In 2010, we were busy renovating a house when my eldest brother suggested that due to my mother's advancing years and increasing frailty we should consider moving to the UK to spend time with her. I was in Africa when my father died in 2002 and I felt I never really knew him as an adult. Not wishing to repeat history I returned to England with Greg to start a new chapter.

I had been away since 1999 and the scared mixed up girl that left was worlds apart from the confident happier woman that returned. We didn't know how long we were returning for or what life was going to be like. It was great to reconnect with family and friends and we both settled into work. I continued to grow and learn which, although challenging, was also amazing and life felt really good again.

Then In 2011, Greg's sister became pregnant after one single round of IVF using donor sperm! I tried to be nothing but happy for her. I really did! But the truth is it rocked me to the core; absolutely shattered me. How can I try so hard and still have no baby when it is so easy for others? The pain was immeasurable and showed that I hadn't come as far as I thought in terms of healing.

This was the catalyst for me to know it was time to truly let go. Enough of the pain and the fruitless trying, it was time to be happy, to live life in the present, live life to its fullest potential and to be happy with everything I did have. I didn't want to be looking in the rear view mirror all my life, but rather to have present moment awareness and live a life worth living and have fun. Over the next year I worked so hard on myself to be clear, free, happy, and to finally let go. It took time, but was the best thing I ever did! No more anger and resentment directed at Greg. We started to have fun together and enjoy each other's company again. As we became closer our relationship grew and it felt amazing that rather than destroying us the past eight years had made us stronger.

Life is a great teacher.

Towards the end of 2014, I wasn't feeling well. Being a healthy lady, I didn't worry too much however by mid-November I was still feeling ill with low energy, constant tiredness, and other flu like symptoms. My menstrual cycle had also stopped and it dawned on me that at 45 years old I was menopausal so I went to the doctor for advice.

I left in total shock! Pregnant! Pregnant naturally at the age of 45! How can that be after all those years of trying so hard? Did I even want a baby now after I had worked so hard to gain acceptance? After learning to fully live my life on my terms and advance my career which enabled me to help many people and make a real difference?

Filled with these confusing and conflicting thoughts and emotions and still not believing it was possible we went for my twelve week scan on Jan 9th 2015 and saw our little being, no bigger than a peanut on the screen. This is real! Emotion welled up within me, but five minutes later we were told that there was an abnormality, that there could be chromosomal issues and that my age was against us. Total shock and devastation followed, I was still getting over the fact I was pregnant and now there is a problem. I was not ready to hear that, but it was a reality I had to deal with.

I drew on all my learnings to release all negativity and stress from my body and worked on some deep inner healing work. I realised just how much I did want this baby.

As I write this, our apparently perfectly healthy baby girl is due in 3 weeks. She is kicking right now.

The impossible was made possible.

To the reader: all that you seek is already within you. When you truly heal your core emotions all that you want can come to you. Be the change you wish to see and believe in yourself because you're worth believing in.

Lynn Jones

Lynn is a woman of courage, who inspires others with her amazing life story. Her health and life collapsed after being harmed by the medical profession, but transformed by becoming an expert in self-help. Suffering has led to a wealth of understanding on the nature of abuse and the healing power of love.

Through self-directed learning, Lynn works to promote a better and safer way of working for medical students. Through writing and speaking, Lynn works to reduce abuse, promote love and empower people to redress the balance of power. Lynn is a life coach, helping personal growth and change.

You can reach Lynn at:

E-mail:
jones_m_lynn@hotmail.com

Warning - Doctors Can Seriously Damage Your Health
By Lynn Jones

At the age of 67, I feel happier than I have ever felt in my life. As my husband and I sat in the sun watching our baby grandson playing, it seemed impossible to feel any better than I felt at that moment. No exotic place in the world or personal achievement could top the bliss from this simple pleasure. It is amazing to think that after enduring the agony of emptiness, loneliness, and despair, I could be living with this level of love, joy, and fulfilment. The incredible thing is that on an almost daily basis I now notice some small change within myself that greatly enriches my life.

In 1976, at the age of 28, I started my second pregnancy. A fear started to rise. After the first birth I was anxious about having stitches out, so to help the head nurse provided gas and air that she didn't switch on and took the stitches out with no sedation. This escalated my fear for the second birth and I set out to get reassurance by mentioning it at the first anti-natal visit. The GP was a young locum, who said it would be no problem to give me soluble stitches after the birth if they were needed. The locum became a partner in the practice and attended the birth, so I felt I would get the care I deserved. He went back on his word and for the second time I was deceived, not only by the GP, but also the nursing staff who once more went through pretence by giving me a Valium injection they said wasn't working, with more gas and air that was not connected, manhandling me into position to take the stitches out, despite my objections.

I had an emotional collapse and cried to the point of exhaustion from the shock, falling into a deep sleep, where nursing staff took over my baby's next two feeds. If things were not bad enough, when I got home I bled and was distraught at the thought of more problems. Needing support from my husband, I turned to him only to suffer more feelings of betrayed trust when he denied paternity for no reason. My husband's behaviour left me heartbroken, with feelings of loneliness, emptiness, and despair. Lost and confused, I suffered further indignities of stigma and shame as a divorcee, after breaking up with my husband to remove myself from emotional agony and suicidal feelings.

As a result of the intrusive medical experience, I suffered Post Traumatic Stress Disorder and was left traumatised. I had repressed the cause within my subconscious awareness, and the medical profession saw me as irrational and neurotic when I had a nervous breakdown, yet I was in touch with reality.

Life was hard with no money or car. My baby boys gave me motivation to hold up in life and a reason to live. Considering the pain and weight of the emotional baggage, I did well to survive as a lone parent. My mother and father were supportive, travelling across town twice a week with a food parcel to visit and help.

In 1982, I met Geoff and we married in 1983. The important thing for Geoff and I was family. It was wonderful for both of us to be a family unit.

A month before getting married, I started a supervisory job, setting up a community aid team to visit elderly and housebound people, while giving long-term unemployed up to a year's work opportunity. Starting with just a note pad and pen, I found my natural intelligence, liaising with social and other services to fill gaps, provide a worthy care service, and a high number of staff found employment within the year.

I was promoted to Senior Supervisor and my team expanded from 12 to 60 people, providing a service described 'as professional as possible for a non-professional group'. From my experience, I had set up a visionary approach to care.

After four years, rumour went round that management was creaming thousands of pounds from the community programme. I developed an obsession to understand what was happening, as I had put my heart into this work, using it as compensation for the heart-breaking belief I had let my family and babies down by not holding up. With my thoughts going at high speed and no sleep, I suffered the first of three episodes of psychosis, which meant a new breakdown where I lost touch with reality.

It was after the second psychotic episode that I realised my great fear and break down was because I had been sexually abused in childhood, which meant that when the doctor put me through the phobia, I re-experienced the trauma of sexual abuse at the emotional age it happened, with no understanding of the cause or my distressed reactions. With sex as a an expression of love and all that is creative on the one hand and all that can cause abuse and destruction to people's lives on the other, I set out to understand the duality of love and abuse.

My early interests in commerce changed to interest in people and social studies. I attended low brow psychology and sociology events with local education groups. After reading the first page of an 'O' level sociology book, I had no understanding of what was written. From there, I attended classes and read a vast number of pop psychology books where I noticed a spiritual theme running through many of them.

Motivational CDs have made an incredible difference to my self-development. My life journey might be described as 'from the pits to the Ritz', where wisdom teachings touched me at the depths of suffering, are with me now, and will continue as part of being a life-long learner.

One line quotes have for many years had a profound effect on me, most memorably, 'If you do what you have always done, you will get what you always got'. With sexual and emotional abuse in my background, change was very important to me. Another significant quote was, 'If you want to change the world, change yourself, as everything changes relative'. This has proved very true for me and my world is totally different. The thing that goes with change is that we lose relationships. One example is when people give up drugs they spend less time with others who take drugs, which is positive. The difficulty comes when the people we need to lose are the ones we love and are significant in our lives. It is then we realise the truth of the saying, 'If we can't say no in the family, we have to say no to the family'.

So, what am I doing now?

Educationally, I am self-taught, having meandered through the fields of social science, using integrity as my yard stick, while I tested truths within the study on myself. I joined The Coaching Academy to become a life coach and after being frozen with fear at the written test, was thrilled to pass with a distinction, which helped to contradict the negative messages of the past from my family that I was "dim and stupid."

I joined Toast Masters International and fast tracked through to gain Competent Communicator. With competence in speaking, I approached a local university to talk to students. An opening became available and I gave talks on the importance of therapeutic relationships using client centred approach and client perspective in mental health. I am able to give students a meditation to show what psychosis was to me with insight into the experience of living with psychosis. I was especially pleased to work with student doctors on the subject of Asperger's and how to identify it in others who have been misunderstood, misjudged, mistreated, and, like me, have slipped the net.

Having studied the depths of human nature for 38 years, I have a vast store of knowledge. From the books in the university library, I now realise that what we learn from outside of self is belief, but what we experience for ourselves is knowledge. Another expression that has meaning for me is 'What got me to this point will not get me to where I need to go'. Progress is about entering new leagues and new dimensions that bring us up against faulty beliefs to break them down and to face fears to overcome so that the potentiality we are born with may flower.

The most momentous thing I have learned about myself is that I am not the person my family and society cast me as. As the youngest female in a working class family, it was my place to be last and certainly not to outshine people with a position of significance. It was not my place to think or to question, but to go along with those bestowed with power and position to make decisions.

For many years my work has been fuelled by belief in what I was doing and the need to right some terrible wrongs from the past. It is the emergence of self-belief that has freed me to move out from an oppressive rank and file way of life, to speak out and show others that with self-belief it is amazing what can be accomplished.

Marie Wood D'Silva

Marie Wood D'Silva is a Transformational Coach and Clinical Hypnotherapist. Marie specialises in Hypnotherapy and Virtual Gastric Band but also uses other modalities like The LifeLine Technique, Energy Healing, CBT, Emotion Code, Focusing and EFT to name a few.

Marie suffered with Depression, Anxiety, and Fibromyalgia for many years, and having used the above mentioned modalities, combined with the support of so many, prayer and a deep commitment to recover, she released herself from the shackles of her invisible illness. She now teaches her clients to do the same.

Marie hopes that by sharing her experience and the tools she used, she can help others recover and improve every aspect of their life.

For more information and to download Marie's free meditation you can reach her at:

Website:
www.mariesmbwc.com

Email:

marie@mariesmbwc.com

Facebook:

https://www.facebook.com/MariesMBWC

From Despair I Found Purpose
By Marie Wood D'Silva

After I had a blackout on December 2nd of 2006, numerous tests and examinations were conducted. As nature would have it, we did find substantial physical issues to keep us steered away from the mental issues. I was yet to discover that this was just the beginning of a dreadful, rocky path, and I was completely oblivious to what lay ahead.

As the days went by, there was always another reason for my mental and physical health to deteriorate. They started mounding on me one enormous boulder at a time until I reached a point where I was no longer able to get out of bed in the morning. My pain and inability to lift my limbs or open my eyes made me secretly wish to be relieved of my earthly duties. I imagined that would soon happen in some mysterious and magical way. I was soon crying on a daily basis, getting deeper and deeper into a dump. Nothing could have prepared me for this.

I had a husband that loved me unconditionally, 2 adorable sons, a helpful mother, supportive family and friends, all of which some people can only dream of. Despite this I was miserable and alone, consumed with my own despair. Not a soul was aware of the depth of my pain, every part of my body was sore and a greater part of it was even sore to touch. I was having gaps in my memory, if I ever got some sleep I woke up more tired, sore and stiff. It took a huge effort to even have a shower, but the emotional pain was what drove me into the ground, that made me weep and want to die.

I remember lying distressed on the floor of my bedroom one afternoon evaluating whether it was time to call my sister, whether it was time to let anyone in on the seriousness and significance of my desolation. Besides the fact that I was not someone you would have expected to be depressed, I felt ashamed and alone, terrified of being known to have a taboo condition. If this was a visible physical injury I'm sure people would understand. I wasn't prepared to hear responses like "snap out of it", "it's all in your mind" or "you have everything, what could you possibly be depressed about?" To be quite honest, I could have possibly thought those same words about someone else not so long ago.

My business as a migration agent eventually took the back seat as I undertook several more tests and examinations, and saw several doctors and medical specialists. Each trip to the doctor or specialist for results only increased the anxiety, pain and panic attacks. Anticipating the words "its Cancer and you have 6 months to live" or "it's a brain tumour" or "you need an operation' hounded me like a pack of vicious wolves... but the diagnosis of several small health conditions kept emerging till it led to the bigger and harder to resolve Clinical Depression, Anxiety, and then finally... Fibromyalgia. I was told that I can expect this condition to last for life, there was no cure; with utter disbelief I waited months to see a 2nd specialist who only reconfirmed the original diagnosis.

I was now secretly wishing to exchange this for a condition that could be surgically removed... I was referred to a pain management program, which did help to a certain degree. I was also referred to a psychologist, but I didn't have the courage to open up to anyone and have that kind of therapy. I was soon 'therapy hopping'.

As time went by, I saw medical specialists, physiotherapists, massage therapists, chiropractors, healers and many more. While all the therapy I had did contribute in some small or big way, it was all a temporary fix for a much bigger needed solution. I soon realised that I was looking for a magic wand, I didn't want to look within, to do the work and allow the healing to occur. Sooner or later my mind caught up with my body and I began to see reality. I was not going to recover if I didn't make the effort, I had to make a firm decision with an unbending intention and deep commitment to recover, and a magic wand was not going to make its appearance, let alone work for me.

I began reading self-help books, listening to Hay House Radio and magically took to it's popular authors like Dr. Wayne W. Dyer, Dr. Brian L. Weiss, Cheryl Richardson, Marianne Williamson, Iyanla Vanzant and Deborah King to name a few. I listened to podcasts by Richard and "Laugh or go Crazy" hosted by Michele & Steve. Dr. Darren Weissman's LifeLine Technique taught me how the subconscious and conscious mind worked. I started to meditate twice a day on a daily basis. I saw a hypnotherapist and was wrapped by his genius. I knew that it would all soon come together, it wasn't the end of the rocky path but, I was starting to see hope for a better future.

I got better and then worse, and this continued for a few years. It did help greatly when I tuned into my progress every so often and checked how far I had come. Every time I looked back it was as though someone just turned on the light. I had cleared so much emotional baggage, baggage that so many of us unknowingly carry from childhood and accumulate over the years.

During that time I learned a few modalities to pick myself up and cope, which I practice myself, and teach or practice on my clients. Some of them are... Hypnotherapy, The LifeLine Technique,

Emotional Freedom Technique, Energy Healing, Focusing, Emotion Code, CBT, Aromatherapy, Sound therapy, Visualisation, and FootDetox. What formed the foundation for my recovery was Meditation and Prayer. I formed a deep and meaningful connection with the Almighty. My daily prayer became the Serenity Prayer "God grant me the serenity to accept the things I cannot change, Courage to change the things I can and the Wisdom to know the difference."

As I got better in grasping all of the modalities and practices and, knowing I had a great support team, I decided to go off my medication irrespective of the medical diagnoses. Once I made that decision I never turned back, I started by skipping my medication one day a week and did this for a couple of months, then I skipped two days a week and gave my body a month to adjust. Soon I reduced the dose of the other days one by one, always making sure my body had fully adjusted before I reduced it even more.

Although it took me 7 months to wean off my medication, I am proud to say that as of the 2nd Feb 2015 I ceased all long term medication. I am thankful for the medication along with everything and everyone that helped keep me alive, because, in hindsight I could say that unattended depression and anxiety is what contributed to Fibromyalgia.

Even though I know the road ahead is not always going to be smooth, surely sadness and happiness will both find its way, I am confident with the tools and practices I have in place. They will help me so that sadness doesn't last longer than it should, and happiness keeps me in form to fulfill my ultimate purpose.

I learned so much during that time:

- I found my purpose and learned to take all obstacles as lessons and difficult people as teachers placed along our path to shape our inner mind and direct our course so that we fulfill our ultimate purpose on earth.

- I found 'meaning' in my suffering. As badly as it pained at the time, I can say that I wouldn't change who I have become, or the choices I made and struggles I went through. All of which placed me in a position to help others, I had to know how it felt at rock bottom, in order to now help others in that place.

- To be responsible for my life and happiness, and allow others to shape their own happiness. To not let irrelevant circumstances dictate how sad or happy I should be.

- To "allow" where necessary, resistance only causes physical and mental pain.

- Self-bullying is counter-productive. I need to be compassionate, encouraging, kind and patient towards myself.

- We do not need to accept a condition for life, we need to prepare and then rely on our instincts to tell us when to hold on and when to let go.

- Most of all, I learned to be compassionate and non-judgmental, to accept that we are all here on our own individual journey to learn individual lessons but as a collective consciousness.

Apart from the aforementioned modalities, this is what gets me by:

Daily - Prayer, Meditation, Gratitude, Yoga (Stretching), Pilates, drinking plenty of water, natural supplements, singing, listening to music, remembering my goals/my purpose, giving people my time for free, reading/listening to inspiring people, activating the 5 senses via relaxing oils & fragrances, colours, sounds, massage and teas, eating the right quantity of nutritious food, journaling, visualisation, mindfulness, positive affirmations, and most importantly the people I love.

Weekly/Biweekly - Being in nature, dancing/swimming/ cycling.

Monthly/Bimonthly - Small adventures/challenges, Body cleanse (FootDetox).

"Nobody is perfect, it is only the imperfect that inhabit the earth, therefore, we must learn to acknowledge our imperfections, accept and correct them, and then accept those of others while allowing them to correct theirs."

Mark Brimson

Mark lives in Bristol and is Director of Payment First, a growing company providing payment solutions to businesses. His dream is to create a thriving national company and he brings passion and enthusiasm to the team.

Mark is an avid Gashead, supporting Bristol Rovers through their highs and lows and gets to every game he can.

Mark's life changed forever when his wife Glo passed away and credits his family and friends with helping him to carry on with life. He now helps and supports friends in similar situations.

You can reach Mark at:

Email:
Mark.brimson@paymentfirst.co.uk

Website:
www.paymentfirst.co.uk

Gloria
By Mark Brimson

She was working as a waitress in a Bowling Alley when I first met her, not as catchy as the song, but a true story none the less.

It was 1995 and I was on a jolly boys holiday to Jersey with 3 of my friends, when one evening we decided we would go to the Jersey Bowl for a bite to eat! We sat at our table and were served by this amazing dose of Irish happiness. Her name was Gloria and for the next few hours she transformed my world.

Fast-forward a month and we got together. At this point in my life I was living in my home town of Bristol and flying over once a month, then every 3 weeks, every 2 weeks and before I knew what was happening I was going every weekend to see her, so we made the decision that I should simply move there to protect the ozone and my wallet.

Life stayed that way until we decided that we should look to get our own place together and therefore move back to Bristol where I was fortunate to get my old job back again. We married in 2000 in her hometown of Killybegs in Co Donegal Ireland and life was great, we enjoyed our DINK (Double Income No Kids) lifestyle and loved to travel together.

On one of our trips to Australia, Gloria started to complain about having headaches, but we just put that down to overexertion and the fact that we had just spent a heavy evening in Sydney celebrating New Year's Eve in style. A few days later though the headaches persisted, so we decided to get these checked out. At

Sydney Hospital and to our relief they too thought she had overdone it with all the flying and late nights we had been having up until that point so we left there with nothing other than some hydrating tablets for her to take.

6 weeks later back in England again the headaches persisted and by now I was getting more and more concerned about it, so she headed for our local GP who was as much use as a chocolate teapot and simply told her to keep taking the aspirin and you'll probably be ok!!

That was my final straw and we decided that we would go down the route of private healthcare and pay for a MRI scan ourselves so at least we could put to bed any worries that it could be anything too serious.

The MRI scan came and went and then the big day arrived when we sat in the consultant's office for him to tell us that we had been worrying about nothing and go back to your lives and plan your next holiday!

Unfortunately that wasn't what he told us, to be honest looking back now that meeting was all a bit of a blur and all I really remember was that the hospital consultant would be in touch soon to discuss the options. What he had actually said I later found out was that although he didn't think there was anything to worry about, there was a cluster of abnormal blood vessels on her brain, which is known as an AVM (Arteriovenous Malformation).

At that time life was a bit of a daze as we met consultant after consultant and each one gave their own take on what should or shouldn't happen, but then we found a guy by the name of Dr Porter who was luckily based in Bristol and seemed to really know his stuff.

One of the first things I learned about an AVM was that it was a condition that you are born with and that the chance of something unpleasant happening increases by 2% a year. In real terms, this meant that by the time Gloria was 50 she was guaranteed a Brain Haemorrhage or worse. We were given 4 options to consider

1. Do nothing, which in all honestly wasn't really an option.

2. Have Radiotherapy on the affected area, then wait for 2 years to see if it had worked, again not really much of an option.

3. 3Embolization, which effectively meant gluing down the affected area until it was a nice hard mass and therefore stopping the potential bleed on the brain – then a year's wait to see results.

4. Have full on brain surgery cutting out the affected area.

We spent about a year researching, talking to doctors all over the country, and eventually decided to go down the route of Brain Surgery as we felt we really didn't want her to go through a procedure then have to wait a minimum of a year to see if it would be ok. Dr Porter had decided he wanted to do the Embolization too so when he did the surgery it should be easier to cut out the mass.

Two weeks before the main surgery she had the Embolization done and all went well and on June 5th 2007 Gloria underwent a 13 hour operation on her brain to get the rest out. This was by a million miles the longest day of my life, I just didn't know what to do with myself.

That night Dr Porter called me and his words went like this "Mr. Brimson, things haven't gone exactly according to plan." Now I was out of my mind with worry, basically what had happened was she had a bleed during the operation which had complicated everything. The next day, I went in to see her and although groggy she was able to recognise me, knew where she was, what day it was and she even knew that I was late! Everything was good there. That evening things were exactly the same and she was stabilizing; everyone was happy.

The next morning at 4am, my phone rang and that is never good news, it had transpired that during the night Gloria had suffered a huge heart attack that she was never to recover from.

So that was me, 32 years of age, widowed and without my soulmate!

There was no book on what I was supposed to do next, although everyone went out of their way to tell me how I should be feeling and what I should do next. In fact the only real piece of good advice I got was from my dad, who told me to make no decisions for a year! The reason I know that it's good advice is because I ignored it.

After taking Gloria home to Ireland to her final resting place (a decision that she would 100% of wanted, but one that has haunted me ever since), I found it really hard to be in the house. Every time I walked through the door I saw her standing in the kitchen cooking, so I decided I would change the house. I put in a Kitchen Diner, put wood flooring throughout the house because it all needed doing.

The reality of course was it didn't need doing at all and after I finished doing the whole house - guess what I still saw her standing there!

I eventually sold the house - another decision I shouldn't have made. I made lots of bad calls at this time; one of the worst was deciding that I wanted a weekend retreat in Spain. I flew over with a friend put £6k down as a deposit then came home, promptly changed my mind and lost the money. You can see now why I now know that dad's advice was good. I was in a really tough spot, huge bouts of depression coupled with really not wanting to live anymore; I simply couldn't see the point in living.

To try to change things, I decided after buying a cricket magazine that I would go to New Zealand to watch England play on a tour. It was here that I vividly remember being in the Bay of Islands sitting on beach with a volcano to my right, golden sand, and the bluest sea I had ever seen in front of me and it was in that moment that I decided that life was worth living after all. What better way to honour Gloria's life than to carry on and try to do the things she didn't manage to.

I tried all sorts when I was home to try to get myself sorted, I tried counselling that didn't work for me at all...I felt like I was counselling the counsellor. I was prepared to try anything at this point and when somebody suggested Reiki, I didn't even know what it was. This however had the desired effect on me, I don't understand it and to be honest I don't want to. I just know now that it works and more importantly I know when I need it next, it really helps me to get my mind back in touch with the rest of me.

Life has moved on considerably in the 8 years since Gloria died. At the time of writing, I am a Sales Director for a Merchant Services company and we specialise in helping businesses save money on getting paid.

In 2013, my beautiful daughter Niamh Lilly was born. I cannot express enough how that young lady has made a difference to my life; she had brought a calming influence that I hope that she will never understand.

One last thing I have learned along the way whilst the pain of Gloria's death remains with me: you can do nothing about what went on yesterday, but you can make a huge difference about what happens tomorrow. Oh and listen to your dad - they may be old and doddery, but they have your best interests at heart!

Mofoluwaso Ilevbare

Mofoluwaso Ilevbare (Fofo) is a REVAMP Life & Leadership Coach, Speaker & Trainer.

Her life oozes energy, passion and a desire to see every little girl, teen, and woman soar, free to fly above all cultural, social, physical & emotional limits, and live her fullest potential.

Having overcome underlying beliefs, life challenges, and two near-death experiences, Fofo's heart beats for "living every day with no regrets". Her legacy will be "Fear Less. Press Forward. Live Your Purpose".

A social entrepreneur & women-in-leadership advocate, Fofo champions a charity for empowering women and young girls in Africa and around the world. She loves God, loves life, and loves to bring out the best in others.

You can reach Fofo at:

E-mail:
fofoilev@gmail.com

LinkedIn:
https://www.linkedin.com/in/mofoluwasoilevbare

Blog:
http://www.lifecoachingwithfofo.com/

Website:
http://www.johncmaxwellgroup.com/mofoluwasoilevbare

Facebook:
https://www.facebook.com/fofoilev

My Blanket Of Fear
By Mofoluwaso Ilevbare

The moment I heard the screeching sound of the tires and felt the car come to a halt, I knew something was wrong. The next thing I experienced was the car moving backwards in a reverse mode, at a speed I could compare to any of the scenes in the movie "Fast & Furious". Suddenly, the noise worsened with the loud sounds of gun shots into the air. Instantly, I bent my head over my lap, my heart pounding, like it would rip out of its cage. My body temperature rose, and my hands trembled with fear. The driver turned off the engine of the car abruptly, after running into a big truck lying on its side by the edge of the highway. The next thing I remember was seeing the driver abandon me, the car, even his shoes, running away from the scene, barefoot.

I turned and watched as his 6ft figure disappeared into the forest. What just happened? "Wake up! Wake up!" I gave myself a hard pinch. "It's only a dream", but the harder I pinched myself, the closer the terrifying sounds of the gun shots kept me in the reality of my situation. Then, I raised my head slightly and looked around. The car was jammed in the midst of several other cars on the highway, most of them abandoned by the owners, people running helter-skelter. I could see a 14-seater bus, full of travellers, lying on its back, turned upside down in a ditch to my left. "Somebody wake me up, this can't be happening. Not today, not now, not to me" I said over and over again. The sight of the pair of brown leather sandals lying at the pedals of the car reminded me that, only a few seconds ago, I had a driver. Where was he? Why would he leave me here despite the security briefing he was trained on?

The day had started beautifully. I jumped out of bed the moment I heard the beeping sound of the alarm clock. I couldn't afford to be late. We had just closed a fabulous business year and this was the day we were having the grand dinner celebration and awards ceremony, our very own "Grammies".

My husband had just bought me a lovely mint-green trouser suit from Argos catalogue and I couldn't wait to launch it on this special night. I had my hair do, woven with African braids, all tucked in the middle into what we call "suku".

We were only half an hour into what would have been an uneventful two-hour drive when I heard the screeching sound.

Back to my reality...my lips were numb. The only words I could muster were "Though I walk through the valley of the shadow of death, I shall fear no evil. God is with me. This is not the day, not now, not me". The gunshots got louder and I knew they were coming closer. I could see about 5 armed gun men, and I watched as two of them literally dragged an elderly man and his wife out of their car, shouting at them, ransacking their pockets and the car. Then it hit me, in less than 10 minutes, this could be happening to me. "God help me. Give me strength" I cried. As I did that, I felt courage well up inside me. I took off my shoes, opened the door on my side slightly, and slipped out onto the ground on the highway. I bent my head for fear of stray bullets, and manoeuvred in between the chaos all around me. I heard one of the armed robbers shout, "Hey you, stop!"

Before my brain could process the word "Stop!" I had scaled over a big ditch and crossed the highway to the other side of the road - gunshots behind me. I felt a bullet fly past me, my eyes got hazy, but all I did was run. Landing on the other side of the road, I ran into the thick forest. The soles of my feet hurt but I would not stop. The thorns tore at my skin but I would not stop. By now my 'straight out of Argos' mint green trouser suit was no longer a suit, it looked more like a rag. Through the chaos, all I kept mustering was "Though I walk through the valley of the shadow of death, I will fear no evil. This is not the day, not here, not now, not me". I don't know how far I ran, but it may qualify me for a half marathon someday. I listened again, still hearing some footsteps in the distance, gunshot sounds. Then all of a sudden, my legs weakened under me. I had no strength left in me to go on, and I fell to the ground with the last breath in me, landing on an abandoned ant hill in the middle of nowhere.

I closed my eyes tightly and muttered over and over again, under my breath "Though I walk through the valley of the shadow of death, I will fear no evil. God is with me. Today is not the day, not here, not now, not me".

I flung my arms tightly around my upper body, as if covering myself with an imaginary blanket. I buried my head in my arms muttering my prayers over and over again. The seconds passed into minutes and then hours. When I finally managed to lift up my head, I could hear cars passing by again, one at a time, the sun had gone down and it was dark. As I listened intensely, the footsteps were gone; the gunshot sounds were no more. Maybe it was time to find my way back home.

I pulled myself up, my feet covered in blood from the cuts and blisters. The adrenalin that flowed through my veins was long gone, replaced instead with aches and pain. A brown muddy jacket, that once was a 'must have' designer outfit, hung tightly to my smelling haggard body. I tiptoed slowly and dragged my tired body out of the forest onto the main road.

With no money, no phone, no identity, I knew I stood little or no chance to hitch a free ride. Yet, I stretched out my hand and waved. Finally, my good Samaritans were scantily dressed cattlemen in a big truck carrying animal manure. They dropped me off at the closest police station. Tears streamed down my face as I narrated my story to the officer on duty.

Two hours later, a familiar face that I longed to see arrived. It was my husband. I looked up on the wall at the clock and realized 8 hours had gone by from the moment I heard the screech. He took me home.

For days, I would not leave the house. A blanket of fear enveloped me. The images haunted me in my sleep. Many times I woke up in the night mustering "Though I walk through the valley of the shadow of death, I will fear no evil for God is with me".

One day, as I said those words aloud, I thought to myself, "If you will fear no evil, why are you still hiding indoors, letting go of your life, wasting away?" Then it dawned on me that though I mustered the words, I still held on to my blanket of fear. At that moment, I chose to get up, take a shower, dress up in a way I hadn't done in days, look in the mirror and repeat to myself "I will fear no evil". I literally flung the blanket of fear onto the bathroom floor and I stepped out into the sunshine.

What are you afraid of?

Maybe, like me, life's tornado has blown your way. Shattered dreams? Lost all you had, including a loved one? Have you lost your self-trust and doubt if you'll ever be able to pick up the pieces? The good news is: **You're Still Here!** Don't let the disappointments and failures of yesterday rob you of a promising future. It's time to leave your **blanket of fear** behind and embrace your **coat of many colours**.

The Missing Piece in Bouncing Back

Losing control, chasing shadows

Lost in a world that feels upside down

The emptiness of the hour

The deadness of the moment

What in the world am I doing here?

Would someone catch me?

Will someone hold me?

Is anyone listening to the whispers of my heart?

What is that? Do I smell rain?

Yes…..it is rain

Refreshing, Restoring, Reviving

Now I'm resolute within me

I've cried my last tear YESTERDAY

TODAY, I'm open to a new awakening

I'm healing, I'm mending

I may not be able to change YESTERDAY

But I can choose how to mould TODAY

What do I seek? What will I find?

How will it be? What must I do?

The questions linger still on my mind

But forward I must walk

In time, I would run

Goodbye!! YESTERDAY

Thanks for what you taught me

Welcome!! TODAY

Indeed something has changed

My soul is free, my mind relieved

I walk into TOMORROW

And I know "it's going to be okay"

©*Mofoluwaso Ilevbare (extracted from A Voice in the Night)*

Pat Matthews

Pat has been many things throughout her life, from civil servant to stay-at-home mum, to running the accounts and administration for the company she owns with her husband, Gerald, for over 35 years.

Her family has always been her priority – she's been a listening ear for all and has dispensed plenty of sage advice over the years. She's the matriarch of a very close knit and supportive family.

Her family asked her to take part in this book to share some of the experience that has helped them so much over the years, so others could benefit from it too.

You can reach Pat at:

Website:
http://www.m-and-b-engineering.co.uk

E-mail:
mandbeng@gmail.com

Counted Blessings
By Pat Matthews

I have very happy memories of my childhood. My parents must have had really tough times bringing up three children in days of rationing, but as a child we didn't notice such things. It's only later you realise that your mum would go without food herself to give to you and your siblings and of course you believed her when she said she had eaten earlier.

All I remember are the good things. The walks with Mum & Dad after Sunday School, usually around the fields of Weston and Lansdown, up Blind Lane and across Cowslip Bank. Dad would pick watercress from a fresh bubbling spring to bring back for teatime sandwiches to go with the jelly and blancmange and we would pick flowers to take home too.

In those days there were carpets of primroses and cowslips and bluebells in Weston Woods at the far end of Broadmoor Lane. They seem to have disappeared in more recent years; maybe we picked them all!

I remember there was much more snow in the wintertime than we have these days. We would go tobogganing with my dad and often bring back wood from the farm for our coal fire. I have more good memories of evenings around the fire, I remember the toasting fork we used to make toast, sometimes dropping the bread into the fire and having to start again! Of course there was no television in those days...

I remember Christmas mornings, running into Mum and Dad's room for our presents only to be persuaded back to bed, as 'he hadn't been yet'. I later found out that they had got to bed at 2am after finishing the painting and stitching on my beautiful pushchair!

We were awake again at 7am and I still remember my gorgeous pushchair with floral pillows and covers, it had such a lovely smell!

The year of the doll's house Dad made was really special, I'm still not sure where it was hidden. It was 4 feet tall, painted white with a red roof, with 2 floors and furniture throughout. It was large enough for my brother and I to hide in and read stories with a torch!

At that time there were three of us, 2 girls and a boy. After 11 years my parents had a very much unplanned bonny baby boy weighing 10 lbs!

I remember my mother saying she was embarrassed to be pregnant at her age and worried about what people might think. It seems funny now, but it was 1955, she was 35 years old and things were very different then.

My baby brother Nigel brought so much love into our lives and he was very special to us all. I was 13 and thought it the most wonderful present, hurrying home from school for cuddles and delighting in being with him. I was even allowed to 'lay in' on Saturday mornings to give him his bottle while Mum got the housework done. My sister and I fought to feed him, bath him and change his nappies – even the challenging ones!

Nigel was the centre of our family life and we all doted on him. I always feel he brought so much to our lives in those special years and the caravan holidays in Devon hold such wonderful memories.

When I went out to work, I would buy him a present on payday, sometimes clothes or toys, but I loved to spoil him. He was very clever at school and had numerous friends. I remember taking him to see The Jungle Book, just Nigel and me and we danced all the way from the bus to our house singing, "I wanna be like you hoo hoo!"

I got married in 1962 to Gerald and in February 1970 I had Nicola (the compiler of this book), my first baby. It was a long and difficult breach birth where we almost lost her.

Nigel thought the world of Nicola! I spent a lot of time at my Mum's house in the day and Nigel would play with her and give her a cuddle when he came home from school. I remember him walking around nursing and cuddling her the day of her first injection when she really wasn't happy!

On the 14th of September that same year, Nigel had a terrible accident and died in Frenchay hospital from a head injury.

We were all numb with shock. My parents were heartbroken; he was the last child at home and the centre of their lives. They slept the next 6 weeks at our home – nights in their own house were just too upsetting. Days were spent with things to sort and arrangements to be made but generally we were all in a haze. Mum & Dad busied themselves with anything they could, but Nicola gave them a focus and a purpose. They loved her to bits anyway but she really came into her own at that time. She was very 'knowing' and I always said she had been here before!

The day of Nigel's funeral at 7 months old she sat bolt upright in her pram with no cushions – she had never done that before. It's funny the things you remember.

One night shortly after when I was too upset to sleep I sat in the living room and wrote a poem to Nigel. It was a full A4 sheet and the words just came tumbling out. I felt at the time that someone was helping me write this poem. I only ever showed it to my husband, because it was too upsetting and heartfelt to show to my mum. Years later, when I would have shown it to her I couldn't find it, but we both still remember how poignant that poem was.

I still say losing Nigel was the most horrible, difficult thing that has ever happened in my life and find it inconceivable that 'God' or 'The Universe' could have ever needed him as much as we did.

I coped at the time, busy with family life and tried not to talk about Nigel because I couldn't without crying and the only person I would cry in front of was my husband. So I kept my emotions at bay not to upset Mum and Dad even more.

It was 5 years later, in the village with my son Darren in the pushchair, when a lady approached me about Nigel and the floodgates opened. I couldn't speak, I just sobbed and she was so sorry to have upset me. All I could do was mumble an apology through the tears and hurry away.

With hindsight, the lesson I think I learned was that counselling at the time of losing Nigel would have helped all of us. When it was suggested we declined, thinking we would find solace in our own family. We then feared upsetting each other and these emotions were buried so deeply. We think we have dealt with them but they are still there.

With counselling, talking freely to an unconnected person can release a lot of the hurt, anger and sadness and maybe it would have helped us to find peace. As it was, we did our best; we pulled together and took one step after the other. Our family was never the same but we all loved each other dearly and although my parents aren't here today I am proud of my upbringing.

Time is a great healer and the good memories do diminish the bad ones in time, I am glad that I got 14 wonderful years with Nigel rather than not knowing him at all. I constantly count my blessings. I have a wonderful, loving husband of 53 years, 2 lovely children, who make me extremely proud and four gorgeous grandchildren. They have all given me endless love and happiness.

We are all very close and constantly in touch with each other, a day doesn't pass without a visit, call or text. I am very lucky, not only do I get hugs from my husband and children; I also get cuddles from my grandchildren. Even my 14 year old grandson, who does turn his head away in the process, just in case Nanny should give him an embarrassing kiss!

How blessed am I?

Rachel Bainbridge

Rachel is a wife, sister, and friend who has faced adversity head on since her early 20's when she lost her parents; latterly facing a cancer diagnosis 6 weeks before her wedding.

As a seasoned HR Professional, she has had people at the centre of her career for nearly 30 years. Rachel walked away from corporate life in 2009 as her values and integrity were not being honoured and embarked on a journey of "giving back" through her *MoreInspired* consultancy; she's never looked back.

These days she works with both individuals and not-for-profit organisations to achieve their goals and ambitions inspiring them with her passion, vision and "can do" attitude.

You can reach Rachel at:

Email:
moreinspired@virginmedia.com

Facebook:
http://www.facebook.com/rachelbainbridge66

LinkedIn:
https://www.linkedin.com/in/rachelbainbridge1

Anything Is Possible In 4 Weeks
By Rachel Bainbridge

As I sit in my garden enjoying a very warm sunny day I reflect back on how things could have been so very different. How the sun, once my friend, quickly turned into Enemy Number 1. You see I was diagnosed with malignant melanoma in 2013 just weeks before my wedding.

Today, I am healthy, cancer-free, and extremely happily married to the best man in the world. Here's my story.

2013 was going to be a great year. I had met the man of my dreams the previous summer and in May he proposed - yes life was good. My dream of a Christmas wedding was soon to be a reality as we planned our perfect day. 19th December 2013.

The countdown was on.

During a holiday in Turkey in September, I started to feel this inner unease, not with my forthcoming nuptials, but, very weirdly, with the sun. Being of olive skin and dark hair, I never had an issue with the sun before; I only had to look at it and I went brown.

This holiday was different. Something inside was telling me to stay out of the sun.

I had had a largish brown mole on my right thigh for years - yes it was larger than the others, but as you do, I had ignored its existence. It was just something that was there along with the countless other moles and freckles. Now something had changed.

151

As I applied sunscreen to the area, I kept examining the mole. I was sure I could see different colours present and it was no longer a uniform shape. I was due to see the doctor in a few weeks' time; I'd mention it then. The holiday came to an end and my thoughts of it disappeared.

As the doctor completed the examination I was booked in for, I casually asked her to have a look at the mole in question not really expecting anything to come of it. Out came the magnifying glass and after only a quick glance, she said "I am going to refer to you to Dermatology for them to have a look at it" I wracked my brain when asked how long I'd had it - to be honest I had no idea. Years was the only answer I could come up with.

"Now don't be alarmed, but as a precaution I have to refer you as an urgent suspected skin cancer case – so you will be seen as a priority." The only words I heard from the doctor at that moment were "cancer " and "urgent."

The next day on my doormat an appointment letter arrived to see the Dermatology consultant the following week. Boy, I really was a priority. This was serious. The panic truly set in. I felt sick.

I immediately burst into tears. This could not be happening. I feared the worse – I feared I had cancer. I was getting married in 10 weeks. Would I still be able to get married? Would I survive?

The following 7 days passed in a state of complete upset, anger and confusion. I googled, countless times, the signs of skin cancer. I had 3 out of the 5 warning conditions; increase in size, change in shape, and change in colour. I googled many different sites hoping that I would read something different. I never did. The ABCDE signs were present on every page for me to see.

I cried, cried, and cried. I panicked, I was an emotional wreck. My partner kept telling me, "Everything is going to be fine" "Fine?

Fine? How can everything be fine?" I would shout back at him. In the reading of one appointment letter my whole world had collapsed. Even my dream wedding wasn't enough to keep up my spirits and re-focus my mind.

That same week I was coming to the end of a challenging consultancy contract. I needed to think of what I was going to do next workwise. I needed to get a job and earn money. How could I possibly do that? How was I supposed to get through an interview when I all I could do was cry, but I did. In fact I managed to land and start a new job, have surgery and get married all within the space of 4 weeks.

The week between GP and Dermatology appointments was quite frankly hell, I frantically scanned every photo I could find of me which might show my mole and which might give me some indication of its age. How could I have ignored it? How long had I had it? My google searches widened from the symptoms of skin cancer to the different grades of cancer and accompanying prognoses. Everything I read scared me more, yet I read on. My emotions were now at rock bottom. The future was not bright. How could I be deprived of living a long life with the man of my dreams?

Having been through my fair share of tragic events starting with the death of my parents and only grandparent in quick succession in my early twenties, I have been through some very dark times. During the 25 years since those events I focused my life around a more spiritual pathway. For me that is not in the religious sense, but in connection with universal energy.

When I was diagnosed with depression 10 years ago, I sought different ways to deal with my illness. In doing so I wasn't reliant solely on medication and conventional psychotherapy, which I did use, as they have a valid place in aiding recovery.

I became attuned to Reiki to work on myself which was great in giving me back some balance. Through avid reading of many different spiritual texts and wisdoms, I found myself very much drawn to working with angels.

Before my first dermatology appointment, I went to my friend for a Reiki treatment as my energy levels were depleted and I needed to regain some balance. Nicky was amazing. She told me to imagine a gold plaster over my mole surrounded by lovely healing light and energy – I did this religiously. Instead of seeing the mole as some awful "thing" growing on me, I focused love and light on it. I followed up Nicky's treatment with my own Reiki self-treatments.

From that moment on, I reminded myself of what I had already been through and how I came away stronger. I used mantras, positive thinking, and visualisation to help me through this difficult time.

As soon as the mole was removed for biopsy, my life moved on. A huge weight lifted off me and I underwent a huge energy and emotional transformation. I was no longer scared, emotional … I was happy. I hadn't even had the diagnosis at that stage. I continually told myself everything was going to be fine. For me the cancer had been removed.

Clearly you will have gathered from the outset of my story, I was indeed diagnosed with malignant melanoma.

When I was given the diagnosis 2 weeks later, I just said, "Yep, ok"; I didn't get upset or anything. The consultant phoned my GP to check if I was alright as she was worried that I had taken the news too well. Luckily it was the lowest grade cancer and it had been caught in time.

After a 2nd round of precautionary surgery to remove tissue surrounding the mole site and being told that no cells had broken away, I was at last ready to get married. Well I had to be as the wedding was only 9 days away.

Just before my second surgery I was offered and started a new job within the space of 5 days; my positivity was paying off.

My wedding truly was the best day of my life with guests commenting that it was the most relaxed and best wedding they'd been to. Our vows were ever more poignant for what we'd both been through. Ok so my dress was a bit loose as the surgery threw my fittings out, but hey, I am not a very girlie girl anyway, and later in the evening with a wig, hat and boots on, it looked great!

The point here is that I remembered to laugh at things again and to appreciate what I had in terms of my gorgeous husband, family, and friends. There is no substitute for fun and laughter.

Yes I have the physical signs of my illness by way of a scar and a chunk missing from my leg, but do you know what, I call it my shark bite…. the shark came off a lot worse I can tell you.

I have learned to deal with and respect the sun with a few easy common sense precautions. I have been on two sunny holidays since surgery and thoroughly enjoyed them. Oh and spray tans are the way to go!

Seriously though, please get to know your body and your moles; don't be afraid of wasting doctors' time getting them checked out. I was not a typical skin cancer case. Online self-diagnosis is certainly not the way; it can get you into dark places very quickly.

You can definitely come out bouncing from the darkest and most challenging times in life. I am now bouncing higher than ever before and work with individuals who want to do likewise so feel free to get in touch.

In summary:

November 13th – Cancer diagnosis

November 20th – Job offer

November 25th – Start job

November 28th – 2nd surgery

December 19th – Wedding

Anything is possible in 4 weeks.

Sharon Critchlow

Sharon is a successful businesswoman who has achieved high standards of professional recognition both in accountancy and financial services. Recognised as a promising entrepreneur by Business Insider in their 42 Under 42 awards, over the past 16 years Sharon has built a flourishing business whilst helping many others to start their career and progress within their chosen profession.

Sharon is a firm believer in having dreams, believing in yourself and having the determination to achieve your goals. Whilst her business is in Bristol, she is a country girl at heart and lives in North Devon.

You can contact Sharon at:

Email:
Sharon@newgrange.co.uk

LinkedIn:
https://www.linkedin.com/profile/view?id=67098401&trk=hp-identity-name&_mSplash=1

Choosing My Outcome
By Sharon Critchlow

The thought of writing this made me laugh, then cry, then laugh again. I am surrounded by amazing people who have overcome all manner of physical and emotional traumas to truly shine. Cancer, stroke, and abuse have been present in the lives of my dearest friends and I'm blessed that none of those outcomes have been in my life to date. What did I have to bounce back from?

Growing up in a small seaside town in the South West of England I had great summers, countless days on the beach and all the fun experiences that happen when you are a teenager working in cafes and hotels. I also had an ineffective education. In the beginning I didn't realise this, or understand what was wrong. The bullying didn't help, the lack of teaching staff didn't help, but I always felt something else was missing. In the early years I was very shy, I didn't like to say I didn't understand and whilst my confidence grew in many areas, I still couldn't bring myself to admit it, but at 16 I struggled to read.

In the 1980's exams weren't necessary to get a job. My hard working parents were pleased with the few exams I passed and I was congratulated upon my success. At the same time I was all too aware that at times, mum had three jobs and dad worked twelve hours a day. For them, life was a daily struggle to provide for us. Watching people enjoying the lovely yachts in the town marina, having the freedom to travel and experience the world on their own terms seemed an unrealistic dream for me. Totally unobtainable.

At 17 I had a breakthrough; I had an eye test and became the owner of some lovely large bright green glasses. I wore them for the first time when I left the opticians and took the train home. I will always remember the tears in my eyes; for the first time in my life I could read the billboards on the platform. I confess to feeling cheated, but I resolved to tackle the reading issue. It was a slow process at first but daily reading practice ensued and reading is now one of my true pleasures in life. At 18 I left full time education having struggled through college, leaving with low grades in my A levels. I had started to believe that my lack of success was because I had reached my intellectual limit, but deep down that didn't feel right.

I had energy and enthusiasm, but was facing an impossible task. I didn't want a life of financial hardship, so I needed a career with prospects. With reading not being my strong point I went for numbers. I decided to be an accountant. I quickly learned that not everyone will share your vision. Their comments are often a reflection of the restrictions they place on their own lives and their fears for you. I heard that "people like us don't become accountants" and "don't be too disappointed when you fail". One of the great things about having nothing to lose is that you may as well have a go at the unobtainable. As few things are truly unobtainable, and in having a go you never know what you may discover.

In the first few years in work I made many discoveries.

In the beginning I discovered that over a hundred letters to local accountants and solicitors yielded two interviews, at one of which they appeared most disappointed at my female form - they were clearly expecting a chap! In fact, I only got replies to letters signed "S Critchlow", no replies to those letters signed "Miss S Critchlow." I also learned that having the name of my school on my CV was more of a hindrance than a help. However, persistence paid off.

I took a position as a filing clerk in an accountancy practice and filed documents really quickly, so that they would have to teach me something new for the rest of the day. After a summer of filing, and some help from my Mum, I moved to a small firm of accountants that needed someone who was happy to start at the bottom. University wasn't an option for me, so I studied for professional qualifications as I worked, and hit an intellectual brick wall. The books were huge! My ability to learn from them was small!

The one day per week at college reminded me of the frustrations of school and I had a similar result. The exams were three hours each at degree level - one year in and I had passed one exam with fourteen left to go. This clearly wasn't working. I asked my employer if he would fund some weekend courses instead. The budget was tight so I chose a small, less expensive college – 200 miles away. This meant I spent one weekend a month away from home, studying.

In the end it took nearly four years but I'm so glad that I went. I met a trainer who showed me how to learn without re writing the book and how to give the examiners what they wanted. This was a revelation. I practiced past papers and the mind mapping technique of using diagrams to organise information presented on the courses and before long – armed with large sheets of paper and colouring pens - I mastered it. It took me eighteen months to pass the next four exams and two and a half years to pass the next ten. I passed the final three after only three months of study. At 23 I qualified as an Accountant with the Association of Chartered Certified Accountants. (ACCA). For me, it was a major achievement and turning point in my life. From this point I was able to move forward with more confidence, knowledge and pace.

At 23 I could not have predicted that over the next twenty years I would go on to pass more exams, become a member of a number of prestigious organisations and alongside my partners build a multi-million pound business. However, I knew things would be different and be better. What I learned about myself in those years would see me through many tough times ahead. I learned much more than accountancy.

I learned that:

- There is no such thing as setting the bar too high - just keep yourself on track with bite sized achievable goals. Congratulate yourself on each goal achieved, and when you lose the will to carry on – re-cap what you have achieved to date and remind yourself how far you have come.

- Years of not seeing the blackboard at school gave me a wonderful talent to remember the spoken word. This is really useful in meetings and goes to demonstrate that early setbacks can give rise to unique skills!

- I could have been written off at age 18 as having reached the pinnacle of my academic abilities. Whilst the professional exams were much harder than A levels, I learned that exams at 16 and 18 tend to be content based, requiring extensive recall of facts with basic analysis. Whereas the more senior professional exams award more marks for understanding how each of these areas come together and interact. For me my true talents are in problem solving. When I see people who struggle with lower level exams I tell them to stick with it, as they could have a brain that solves problems easily and as the exams progress they can increasingly play to their strengths.

- I have discovered that learning is not a linear thing; you can have a breakthrough at any stage, you may just need a different approach.

- The more I tried, the more people stepped forward to help with the tools I needed. I learned that those who succeed weren't always those with natural talent - more often they were those who wanted it the most and were prepared to keep going – even with a 400 mile round trip.

- Things not going well? Chat over how you feel with someone who has been there before, someone who shares your passion for the project, or someone who shares all of your passions. Let others pace for you to get you across the line. It will still be your success. I have learned to ask for help, and that if you are committed to the outcome, others will help.

- Be patient with those who do not see your vision. Whether it is prejudice against your background or your gender, or well-meaning words which are aimed at protecting you, but deflate your dreams - remember that sometimes the world is just like that. It says everything about them and nothing about you – unless you decide to own it. Whatever you are telling yourself will dictate your future, not whatever they are saying to you - so have faith in your abilities. Only you will truly know how much you want this.

Finally, remember this, the world is full of infinite possibilities and outcomes. With all of those possibilities available to you, you may as well choose your own outcome.

Good luck!

Tim Johnson

Tim Johnson leverages his personal and commercial experience and expertise to help others achieve "authentic success". "Authentic success" means different things for different people. Tim has a fascinating personal story to share…

From losing his arm in a car accident, attaining an MBA, and building two £3m+ businesses Tim's own authentic journey will inspire, empower, and motivate you to action.

Tim enables his clients to count, monitor, and measure the growth they want when following and implementing his approach.

Take time to discover more about Tim, and more importantly how Tim can help you to discover, define, and deliver what success really means for you.

Tim Johnson is founder of "Authentic Success", an innovative coaching and consultancy practice that enables individuals and business owners to discover, define & deliver what it is that they really want. Having completed his own personal journey of discovery, Tim has clearly defined the ways that he can help others achieve their goals and objectives to deliver what success means to them. To find out what "authentic success" can mean for you, contact Tim at tim@autheneticsuccess.co.uk and claim your FREE "authentic success" audit.

You can contact Tim at:

Website:
www.AuthenticSuccess.co.uk

Facebook:
https://www.facebook.com/TurnaroundTim

Twitter:
@TurnaroundTim

LinkedIn:
https://uk.linkedin.com/in/turnaroundtim

Turn Around To A Path Of Authentic Success
By Tim Johnson

The first thing I can remember is standing by the side of the road looking down at my upside down car in the ditch. It is the dead of night on a chill November evening in 2001, the air is still, and I find I'm cradling my right arm with my left, as it appears to flapping from the shoulder and at the elbow. I have no idea how I got out of the car and scrambled up the embankment. Curiously there is no pain.

I wonder what to do next? Shall I scramble back down and retrieve my mobile phone – that doesn't seem possible. Should I hop over the fence and flag down a car on the motorway below? Looking back on it the absurdity of that thought is almost amusing. I wander down this country lane to see if I can find help. I soon come across a cottage and I bang repeatedly on the door. It's around 1:30 am and eventually a brave soul answers. As luck would have it, she is a theatre nurse and she takes me in to her home, lays me down in her hallway and keeps me conscious by talking to me whist we wait for the ambulance to arrive.

The following day the surgeon brings me around on the ward and apologises for amputating my arm at the elbow. For me this is another stroke of luck as I'd assumed I'd lost it at the shoulder. However things start to get tough after that. Weeks of operations, bone grafts, skin grafts, infections, and the dreaded MRSA all took their toll and my business partner terminated my directorship in the middle of this. Overcoming the addiction to opiates is a whole new story!

I was without a job, no income, had a family of 5 to feed and a whacking great mortgage. At one point returning from the hospital, I was so weak that it took me a full 5 minutes to get up a single flight of stairs. At the top of the stairs, I resolved to get fit. That was it, no smart goals here, just compass point direction. By taking small baby steps I got fitter, starting with trying to get to the letterbox at the end of the road and gradually increasing speed and distance day by day, week by week. It wasn't consistent of course, some days were duvet days and others seemed brighter, but 2 years later I found myself doing an Olympic distance triathlon (a mile swim, 26 mile bike ride, and a 10K run) in a half reasonable time. The lesson here is that by taking baby steps in the same direction, using the clear compass point as a guide, you can go further and achieve more than you may have thought possible at the outset.

As it happened the protracted legal battle over the value of my shareholding in the manufacturing business I'd helped take from a failing start up to a £4m turnover market leading business in its niche, went as well as I could have expected. The huge overdraft went to an even larger positive balance even after paying off the mortgage. The surprising thing was I didn't feel as ecstatic about that as I'd expected. The reality was that I'd come to use the litigation battle as my reason to get out of bed in the morning, and the money at the end of the day was just a number on a spreadsheet.

Having said that, it did allow me the time to take an MBA, train as a business coach and a mediator, and set up my own one man band consultancy. I went networking and after a few months found myself helping people with debt solutions too. I also saw how channelling the huge energy of a new business partner could work as we co-founded a new business breakfast network of our own. 5 years later, we'd created a £3m turnover network with full national coverage and a small footprint in Australia. History repeated itself and almost 10 years to the day after losing my arm and my role in the manufacturing business, it was decided that it was time to leave the networking business.

On one hand I thought that's fine, I've been here before, I know the ropes and I can handle this. On the other hand (if I had one!) I relentlessly beat myself for not learning the lesson before and not to take a minority shareholding with a particular type of character.

However it afforded me the opportunity to do business turnaround work and I successfully saved 6 businesses from closure, all of which are now still trading and to start a small property business. But, and it is a big but, I was chasing the money and trying to create residual passive income as we are often encouraged to do. I was disconnected from myself and my heart, and my relationships were suffering too. The pressures compounded and intensified leading to a breakdown of our 22 year marriage.

A move to Bristol to live on my own started the intensification of my personal development journey that had started after the car accident, and was now almost a full time occupation. I reasoned it was pointless to take on bouncing back in my usual determined business focused way if it ultimately didn't create the happiness that I was looking for.

A year later I eventually worked it out – the path to Authentic Success… You see I'd been previously successfully bouncing back through a logical left brained perspective with fear and other people's agenda as the driver. It created results without the long-term pleasure, it was destination focused, not journey enjoying. What I learned was that I needed to get still enough to listen, observe and discover what I wanted at a heart and soul level, get clear about the gifts I can bring to the world, and find the support available to start taking action. This allowed me to develop the Authentic Success Program.

The Authentic Success path is of course individual to each and every one of us, so there is no prescriptive formula, however having a program to work with helps guide you through the 3 core stages of Discover, Define, and Deliver. Conveniently the word 'Authentic' has nine letters allowing 3 letters to each for each part of the framework. In Discover we have Awareness, Understanding, and Themes. In Define we have Happiness, Environment, and Needs. In Deliver we have Take Action, Integrate, and Celebrate. To help you find your own authentic success follow this path:

Awareness. Until we can become aware of our own thoughts, feelings, bodily sensations, intuition, emotions, and energy we can't tap into the amazing GPS our body has for us to guide us on our way.

Understanding. When we learn to quiet our mind enough, so we can listen deeply without the distractions of the chattering mind conjuring up fearful emotions, we can begin to see things for what they are and not get caught up in the stories. We begin to see our true selves.

Themes. As we dis-member the jigsaw pieces from our fixed stories of the past and projections of the future, with a quiet mind we can start to notice themes in our lives, patterns of behaviour and reactions, ways of being and thinking. Without judgement, but by simply noticing and observing, we can gently start to assemble themes that are more in line with how we are now and how we wish to be rather than being stuck with the conditioning of the past.

Happiness is an inside job! Viktor Frankl reminds us in Man's Search for Meaning that it's in creating meaning in and choosing our responses to whatever we are experiencing that makes the difference.

Environment. Having said that happiness is an inside job, your environment and how you respond to it can have an impact. Changing both some factors in your external environment whilst also changing the way you perceive it can deliver dramatically improving results.

Needs. Now you've listened to yourself, unpacked the pieces, reordered them, and sorted out the internal and external work you want to do, what do you need to do? Write a list – it may be a long one or a short one.

Take Action. With a long needs list there is the danger of feeling overwhelmed. Know you are on a path and now that you've set your course with the compass in your hand start taking baby steps. Be gentle on yourself and prioritise your list.

Integrate. Putting all this lot together and living it can be difficult without the reminders and support to do so. I greatly favour Fresh Air Fridays as a growing movement of people to join to help you integrate the changes in to your life. www.freshairfridays.co.uk

Celebrate! What you focus on you get more of. Focus on gratitude for what you have, remember to celebrate the small things along the way and you'll be more used to enjoying life. Enjoy!

Tina Marie Parker

Tina Marie Parker is a business advisor and trouble-shooter that has been helping businesses solve their organisational problems for nearly 30 years. Her company, Nozey Parkers, works with companies from start-up to succession planning. From companies going through rapid growth to companies desperate to see some growth. She helps them thrive and survive. She gives great business advice and hands-on support for SME businesses, getting the desired results, fast.

Tina started Nozey Parkers in 2013 after surviving an abusive first marriage, bringing up a daughter with ADHD, being mum to 2 wonderful step daughters, and marrying the man of her dreams.

Tina is passionate about helping parents with special needs children, by public speaking on the subject, as often as possible. Tina also wants to help women who have been through abusive relationships to thrive and create the life they deserve.

You can reach Tina at:

Website:
www.nozeyparkers.co.uk

Email:
tina.parker@nozeyparkers.co.uk

Twitter:
www.twitter.com/Nozeyparkers

LinkedIn:
https://uk.linkedin.com/in/nozeyparkers

Facebook:
https://www.facebook.com/tina.parker.779

No One Is Perfect
By Tina Marie Parker

I had an idyllic and happy childhood. I lived in a tiny cottage in the woods with my parents and younger brother. Our garden blended with the surrounding countryside so I was always outdoors, climbing trees, makings camps, and watching the wildlife.

I was a perfectionist and always put 100% into everything I did, and I excelled, both in school and with my hobbies.

I was a bit of a performer, I was confident, I picked up things really quickly, but I was not arrogant or big headed with it. I just did my best. All I heard from people were wonderful, positive comments.

My parents have a loving marriage, and are still together and very happy. As a child, I used to dream of meeting my Mr. Right and of the way he would treat me and how happy we would be. At this time I also had a sense that I was not alone and that something or someone was trying to find me.

At the age of 11, just after puberty kicked in, I started to have these recurring dreams of a male figure coming to talk to me, and tell me how much he cared and loved me, and that he had to be with me.

These dreams stopped when I was 19 and I met my first husband. He lived in London and he suggested I move in with him and find work locally.

The first year or two was OK but then he changed. The verbal abuse started – "You're useless" "What culinary shite have you cooked tonight" "You should be thankful I married you" "You are so fat and ugly, no one else would put up with you". It did not matter how hard I tried to get everything perfect it was never good enough for him. He would always find something wrong with anything I did. He would call me derogatory names whilst we were out, in front of our friends. I really felt like a waste of space.

Then he got physical. He was very controlling. Pinning me down. Not letting me go. And then when I had had enough and tried to fight back, he would retaliate, not with the appropriate force, but with full force, leaving me with bruises. He would throw things at me, put his hands round my throat and throw meals at the walls.

So my home life was pretty crap, with me crying myself to sleep most nights, constantly being rejected, dreading him coming home every night, not wanting to live anymore. I was so naïve that I assumed all marriages were that way, and my childhood dreams were just fantasy.

He made me feel so worthless that who else would want me anyway, I was hideous, I was not perfect. I hated going out because I was embarrassed by how hideous I was. I couldn't look people in the eyes either because I did not think it was fair that they had to look at me, when I looked so repulsive. I daren't speak in case something I said might trigger a negative response from him, and anyway, no one would want to hear anything I had to say!

My career started mirroring my home life. So I constantly was getting the message of "you are not good enough". It did not matter how hard I tried it seemed I was being told that it was not good enough. Probably because of the put downs at home, and the way I thought about myself, I was an easy target for a bully at work.

I stayed in the marriage for 16 years. The only good thing to come out of it was my daughter. I did nearly lose her whilst pregnant. My boss at the time bullied me so much that I ended up in hospital 3 times with heavy bleeding.

The marriage fell apart when my daughter was 3 because my first husband started turning his aggression towards her, and it suddenly made me wake up. At this time I had started to have vivid dreams again about the male figure I had dreamed of as a child. This time though he was an adult and very distressed. He kept saying that he could not go on without me. I used to wake from the dreams feeling so desperate and helpless.

I had to get out of my first marriage so I worked out if I could manage financially on my own without my ex, because I was pretty certain he would not give me anything toward my daughter's up keep. I'm glad I did because he has never given me a penny.

My daughter suffers from ADHD/Asperger's. My ex's parting words were "Who's going to want you and that child".

In 2003 I decided to join some dating websites as I had so much to give to someone and felt I had been putting my life on hold for far too long. That's where I met my current husband Andy.

When we met I felt so comfortable with him and felt like we had known each other for years. He had recently gone through a messy divorce, been made redundant and lost his younger brother to cancer. As we got to know each other it became clear that he was the male figure I had dreamt of for all those years!

Andy has been so patient with me over the years we have been together. I thought I was OK when I left my first husband, but I did not realise that the emotional scars my ex had inflicted on me, were still very raw and tender.

Because of the constant put downs from my first husband and the rubber stamping from some terrible bosses, I felt worthless and that anyone who was with me was just with me out of pity. I assumed that Andy was with me just so he had someone. That something is better than nothing. I was so insecure but just accepted my perceived situation for what it was because that was all I deserved.

After meeting Andy I started to remember all the great things I had achieved throughout my life and my perception of me started to improve.

Andy and I have not had it easy. When we met he had twin 9 year old girls to bring up because their mother had walked out. She was an abusive person and both girls have self-harmed and needed counselling as a result of her behaviour.

My daughter's ADHD/Asperger's has made life interesting too, over the years.

In 2014 her Dad, my ex, started to repeat his controlling, physical behaviour with her, but with the schools and Social Services help this has now been dealt with. When my daughter was explaining what my ex was doing to her and they were saying how awful it was, all the emotions that I had felt at the time came flooding back. What was different this time though was I could now see how terrible he had behaved all those years ago. I had not realised it at the time. I had just accepted it and got on with life.

My first husband did his normal controlling thing and would not give me a divorce, so we had to wait 5 years before Andy and I could get married in 2009.

I did not clear out completely all the negative thoughts about myself. I still thought that Andy would ask me to leave at any moment, because I was worthless and I thought he was just waiting for something better. It is still a work in progress, and even when we got married I still thought it was out of pity. Totally irrational I know!

It was not until I took the plunge and went self-employed in 2012 that I really started to get back to more rational thinking about myself. I even used the Nozey part of a teasing name that I was called as a child, with my new surname, to get to Nozey Parkers. I have great attention to detail and am naturally very organised and nosy - all from being a perfectionist at such an early age and then having to make sure everything was as perfect as it could be to minimise the bullying and criticism. The silver lining to my cloud.

I finally can truly be ME. No more treading on egg shells. No more only doing and saying what I think the other person wants to hear. I am just ME and it feels so great!

In the early years of my life all I did was my best. I was not big headed. Then due to always trying to do your best but being told it's not good enough, you try even harder to please. So my thinking was if it's not perfect or I'm not perfect, it's not good enough!

BUT no one is perfect, no situation is perfect, everyone has their faults – and that's OK.

Remember - You are unique. There is no one else like you. Everyone's path, both personal and business, is different. Do not compare yourself with anyone else. Don't ever go there. Your journey is like no one else's.

Don't pay attention to what other people say about you. It is just their opinion and their words. Don't ever take them personally or believe what they say as the truth, as I did for so many years.

Do your best, be yourself and that's always enough.

Conclusion

When I met the bubbly, fun loving lady, Kate Gardner, we enjoyed a fabulous chat. What I didn't realise then was how our meeting would lead me to this incredible journey!

Writing has been a passion of mine all of my life. I have written two of my own books and now co-authored five more with other incredible writers. There is something about reading a book that brings tears and compassion on a whole new level. I co-authored a book that went to the Amazon International Bestseller list within four hours and then I had this opportunity to compile my own Missing Piece book!

Gathering 23 people to work with me on this book was one of my own greatest challenges. This is proof that it's ok to doubt yourself and lose your vision…as long as you pick yourself up and get going again as soon as possible!

I have always known that people are amazing and capable of making huge changes when faced with adversity and challenge. The chapters you have read in this book prove that fact.

My wish is that this book inspires you on a challenging day. That you ask yourself, "What would I do if I knew I couldn't fail?" Gift this book to a friend in need or recount one of the chapters when you know someone should hear that they can do it too.

If you feel inspired to write your story, a poem or a work of fiction – please do it. You never know the inspiration, enjoyment or peace you may bring to another soul on this planet. By shining your light, you give others permission to shine theirs. Together we can illuminate our world!

Nicky Marshall

Discover Your Bounce Today!

Beat Stress!

Sleep Well!

Burst With Energy Every Day!

YOU Can Rediscover Your Bounce!

Visit www.discoveryourbounce.com/BounceBoosts today to arrange your Bounce Boost Session!

Because Your Purpose Is Our Passion!

The End ☺

Lightning Source UK Ltd.
Milton Keynes UK
UKOW06f2102240815

257437UK00002B/53/P